A MANUAL OF
HEAVY
WEATHER
SAILING

JEFF TOGHILL

REED

First published in 1994 by
REED BOOKS
a part of Reed Books Australia
Level 9, North Tower
Chatswood Plaza, 1-5 Railway St.
Chatswood, NSW 2067

National Library of Australia
Cataloguing-in-Publication Data
Toghill, Jeff, 1932 -
A manual of heavy weather sailing
Includes index.
ISBN 0 7301 0409 5
1. Sailing - Handbooks, manuals etc.
2. Heavy weather seamanship, I. Title
797.124

Editor: James Young
Designed by Bruno Grasswill
Illustrations by Bruno Grasswill
Produced in Australia by McPhersons Printing Group

Contents

The sea 65

Wind and weather 75

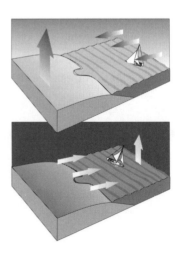

Cyclones, hurricanes and typhoons 91

Preparing for a blow 99

A pre-gale check list 104

Riding it out   **123**

When the chips are down   **139**

Introduction

The ocean is a very unforgiving place, and mistakes made out on the open sea can be costly both in terms of money and of human life. When the chips are down and the ocean has turned nasty, only experience and skill-and perhaps an element of luck-can mean survival.

No matter if it is 1 mile offshore or 100 the problems are similar, albeit not identical. Indeed, 1 mile offshore can often be more dangerous than 100, for the ocean's angry reaction at being constrained by a coastline can reveal a far greater fury than well out at sea where, as master of all, it can be just as angry, but far less vindictive. Statistics show that more vessels come to grief in the immediate waters off the coast than in the wide expanses of open ocean, an aspect of offshore sailing that is as important as it is little known.

But wherever the problem occurs, the outcome can be just as disastrous, and once again survival gets back to the skills and experience of the sailor and his or her ability to cope with whatever the ocean dishes up. Such skills and experience go hand in hand for, to use a biblical term, one begets the other. Skills can only be gained by experience, and experience is only gained when the skills are put into practice.

All of which would make it seem that a book, which involves neither the skills nor experience, is rather superfluous. Yet both skills and experience are dependent on knowledge, and knowledge of the sea, the weather and how the two can combine to make life unpleasant, even life-threatening, is a worthwhile starting point for acquiring both skills and experience.

This book is intended to provide a basic knowledge of factors involved in riding out and surviving storms at sea. Not just factors concerning the elements of wind and sea, but also broader factors which concern the structure of a seaworthy boat and the hull shapes which create the intangible but vital property known as 'seakindliness'. The ways in which the punishment meted out by a storm can best be absorbed with minimal damage and maximum comfort. Factors which all contribute in some way to safety and survival in the face of a savage blow.

From gentle land and sea breezes to the horrendous cyclones and hurricanes, all are examined as a part of the scene involving small craft and the open sea. From forecasting the approach of unpleasant weather to eventually riding out a Force 10 gale, the whole offshore scenario is detailed for boats that are powered by sail or motor, and have single or multi-hulls, boats with the ultimate in electronic equipment and those that carry only a piece of dried seaweed in the rigging. There is only one way to deal with nature when it shows its worst side, and that is in an all-encompassing manner.

The information provided in this book is gleaned from the only reliable source-those who have been out there and done it. While the cover carries the name of only one, the details it contains come from dozens of different sources-all experienced 'blue-water' sailors who have contributed their knowledge in the interests of education and enlightenment of those who follow in their watery footsteps.

CHAPTER 1

What Makes A Seaworthy Boat?

There is often no second chance for the sailor, and the boat taken out to sea is all there is to bring him or her back home. Which surely is the best reason for any sailor, inshore, offshore or ocean-crossing, to ensure that the boat underfoot is capable of doing the job, no matter what conditions wind, weather or sea conspire to produce. Before leaving port the sailor must have total confidence that the craft will cope with anything that crops up during the coming passage, because if it doesn't, then the journey may well end tragically.

So what sort of boat is going to provide security and peace of mind when the sea turns nasty? What features must the sailor be aware of and have checked before leaving the safety of harbour; perhaps before even buying the boat? What is that elusive quality that gives a boat the ability to withstand anything the sea may

Whether cruising or racing, putting out to sea requires a sound, seaworthy boat if the passage is to be safe for all on board.

Most Power boat hulls are designed as a compromise between the sleek, fine lines of a yacht and the stable, but bulky shape of a workboat.

throw at it? In short-what makes a seaworthy boat?

In many ways this is a relatively simple question to answer; in other ways it is not. For example, the pounding and banging of a broad, flat-bottomed, punt-type hull as it thuds across a steep chop leaves no question in the occupants' minds as to whether or not this craft is seaworthy in the conditions being experienced. Comfort alone conveys a very strong message and passengers will happily disembark at the first possible stop to nurse bruised and battered bodies. For this type of sea condition, a blunt, flat-bottomed boat is not seaworthy.

By the same token a slender, pointed hull would cope with the same chop quite effortlessly, slicing through it with no more than a soft thump, thump, and making no attempt to dislodge the occupants' teeth from their jawbones. The chances are the passengers would be quite comfortable and happy to continue the journey for as long as was required.

Now let's take the same two boats in different extreme conditions; this time with the sea on the beam. Now the narrow boat will be in trouble, with almost every sea rolling her onto her beam ends and threatening to capsize her. The broad punt, by contrast, will barely roll at all, coping admirably with the beam seas except, perhaps, for taking some spray aboard as she resists the push of the waves against her sides.

So the punt is a seaworthy boat in terms of stability, but not in terms of sea-riding, while the long, narrow boat cuts through the waves just fine, but is less stable and more vulnerable to beam sea conditions. This is just a basic illustration, but it offers an indication of two of the many ways in which a boat can and cannot be seaworthy. To be able to cope with both conditions satisfactorily, you would need a broad, flat-bottomed, thin, long punt which, of course, is not possible. So compromises are made and most boat designs are just such a compromise.

The basic factors indicated by this example are that a good beam is necessary to provide stability and a fine entry for seakindly performance. The designer has to decide how to combine these two for maximum performance. Plus, of course, a wide range of other factors which affect the boat's sea performance in other ways. This is where the designer's skills come into play: juggling all these factors to produce a hull which will offer the best possible performance in the sea conditions for which it is intended.

In doing so the designer will take into consideration a number of major factors that play an important part in the design of the hull, and which will require special attention. It is worth looking at these factors and the methods adopted to reinforce the hull to counter their effect. Since these are common to all seagoing craft, a wise boat-owner will know all about them and be able to assess how well his or her vessel is designed and built to counter them.

Stresses from the sails are transferred through the mast and rigging to the hull. It is important that these are distributed evenly.

Stresses and strains

The need for special shapes in a boat's hull comes about as a result of the action of different sea conditions on the hull. For example, the effect of driving the bow straight into a sea will cause major stresses to affect the front part of the hull while the stresses caused by the boat corkscrewing across a quartering sea will be quite different and will affect many parts of the hull along its full length.

When under a full press of sail and riding a big sea, there are enormous stresses affecting every part of the hull, and these are aggravated by the stresses created by the driving force of the sails being transferred to the hull through mast and rigging. Under storm conditions these stresses are exaggerated to the extent that unless the hull is designed to withstand each and every one of them,

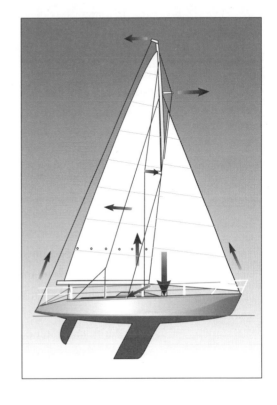

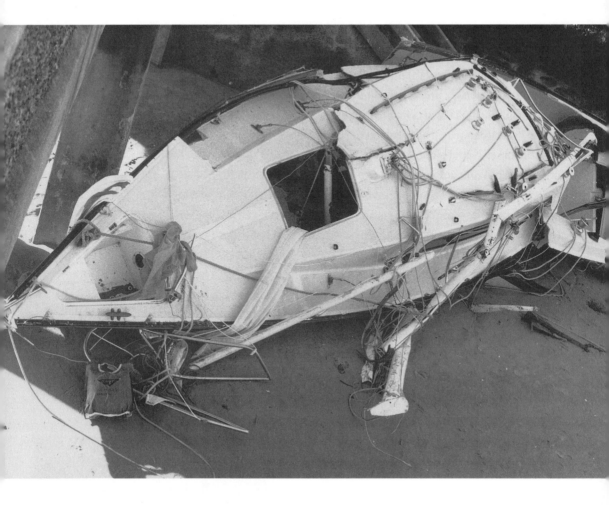

When the stresses and strains are too much for the structure of the hull, it will, like anything else, simply crack up.

the hull will start to break up. The reinforcement mentioned earlier which is built into the hull structure is designed to withstand these stresses, and it is these structural members, when combined into the total hull design, that determine just how seaworthy a hull is.

Knowing how seaworthy a boat will be can be judged to a certain extent by its shape. To use our previous example, it is fairly obvious that the flat-bottomed extreme mentioned earlier will not ride any sort of a sea comfortably. However well built and reinforced it may be, sooner or later it will smash itself to pieces against the sea. So allowing for a reasonable 'seakindly' shape that will ride the seas well and a hull that is well reinforced to withstand the stresses it will encounter in a seaway, some picture of what makes a seaworthy boat begins to appear.

But to understand the full implications of what is required to make a hull seaworthy, it is necessary to understand in more detail the stresses and strains that affect a boat in a seaway.

Panting

When a boat is driven forward into a sea, the bow is buried deep into the face of the wave and enormous pressures come to bear on the front sections of the hull. To begin with there is the impact of striking the wave, which tends to push in the hull skin in the forward areas. Then there is the upward pressure as the buoyancy of the hull forces it up and over the wave and this again adds pressure to the already highly stressed hull skin in the forward areas.

As the bow lifts high out of the sea, cresting the wave prior to crashing down into the next trough, these pressures are immediately relieved and the depressed hull skin springs back to its original shape. A moment later the cycle is repeated as the bow falls into the following trough and the forward sections of the hull are buried deep in the face of the next wave. Since this action may take only a matter of ten or fifteen seconds, the hull skin is subjected to a constant series of flexings as much as half a dozen times a minute.

This is termed 'panting' and places the hull skin at the bow under considerable pressure. Constant flexing of this type can create fatigue in any

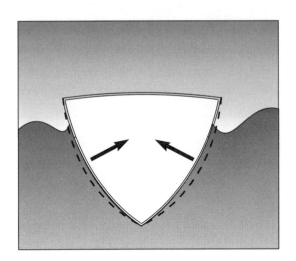 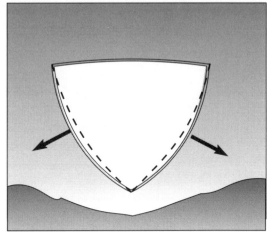

material, as witness the effect of flexing a piece of tin or aluminium for a period of time. Of course, most materials used for boat building are designed to withstand such stresses over a considerable number of years. Nevertheless, in creating the shape of the bow, the designer must bear in mind the need to reduce the effects of panting wherever possible.

This is done by fitting structural members inside the skin at the bow, thus preventing the skin from flexing inwards when the bow is buried in a wave. The forward bulkhead is a major factor in this reinforcement of the bow, as are the

Enormous pressures come to bear on the front sections of the hull which is subjected to a constant series of flexings as the boat ploughs through the water.

15

stringers which run aft from the stem-post inside the hull skin. The bulkhead is usually watertight to prevent the hull from flooding in the event of the bow being damaged in a collision, and this makes it a very strong structural member in an area where strong reinforcement is required.

Pounding

This has an even greater effect on the hull and it is not unknown for the structural members to be so severely stressed when pounding that eventually the boat breaks up. Pounding occurs when the boat moves fast over the crest of a wave, lifting her bow clear and crashing down in the trough with her 'underbelly' taking the worst of the impact.

Yachts are less vulnerable to this problem than power vessels, partly because yachts have a finer entry under the hull (they are not so flat-bottomed) and partly because yachts are usually moving at a slower speed. The worst scenario for severe pounding problems is when a power vessel 'jumps' off the top of a wave and crashes bodily down into the trough.

This can at best cause injury to the crew, at worst it can stove in the bottom of the hull and create serious damage.

The underside of the bow takes most of the impact when a boat crashes down a trough.

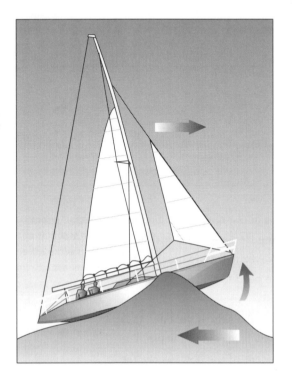

The way to avoid pounding, and to a certain degree panting, is to reduce speed. All boats are designed to cleave the water with their bow and most can generally cope with this quite satisfactorily. But when a boat is driven hard at a wave or projected off the top, the resulting impact jars her structure, risking severe damage to many part of the hull, in particular the bottom structure. Reducing speed causes the boat to ride more gently over the wave and accept the oncoming face more kindly-seakindly!

Hogging

When a boat rides over a wave there is a moment when, figuratively at least, she is poised on the crest with her bow and stern both hanging over the troughs on either side. At this point the entire weight of the boat is supported at a midships point by the upward pressure of the wave, while the bow and stern sag downwards with little or no support. This 'bending' action causes great longitudinal stresses on the main structural members of the hull, creating the situation known as 'hogging'. Carried to its extreme, hogging could theoretically break the boat in two in much the same way as a stick can be broken across a knee.

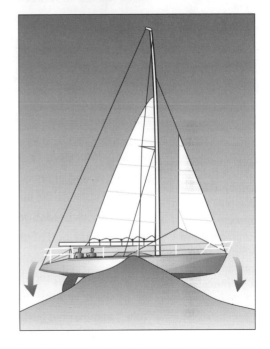

The longitudinal members of the boat's structure form the reinforcing designed to withstand hogging. The main member is the keel or keelson which run along the bottom of the hull. The stringers, at points up the hull, and the beam shelf, at deck level, help to create the rigid 'tube' structure which prevents the hull from bending or breaking. All these members run the length of the hull and are secured at the bow and stern into the stem- and stern-posts respectively.

When a boat rides over a wave there is a moment when she is poised on the crest with her bow and stern both hanging over the troughs on either side. The situation is known as 'hogging'.

Sagging

This is the opposite situation to hogging, where the ends of the hull are supported by two waves, one at each end and the midships sections 'sags' unsupported into the trough. Because waves are rarely the right distance apart to create this situation, it is not as common as hogging. However, the stresses are similar to

Sagging is the opposite situation to hogging, where the ends of the hull are supported by two waves, one at each end and the midships sections 'sags' unsupported into the trough.

those of hogging and the same structural members are used to counter them.

There is not much the crew can do to reduce the tendency of the boat to either hog or sag other than to alter course so that she is crossing the waves at an angle rather than meeting them head-on. In any case, as a general rule, a well-designed boat will be adequately reinforced to cope with such conditions unless they become extreme. In any case, heading at an angle across the waves, especially with a following sea, can induce another, even worse problem called 'wracking'.

Wracking

This is the action which results from the boat working at an angle to the seas, either when heading into them or when running before them. The combined rolling and pitching action of crossing the waves in this manner tends to create a twisting or screwing stress in the hull which can be likened to that induced in a shoebox when its ends are twisted in opposite directions. The shoebox will eventually collapse, and so will the hull of the boat if it is not constructed in a way which resists these stresses and strains.

Just as with the shoebox, the stresses of wracking cause the hull to distort out of shape and this can only be countered by strong stiffeners reinforcing the 'tube' shape of the hull. While almost all structural members come into effect in this situation, the main members which prevent the collapse of the hull are the bulkheads and the beam knees.

Beam knees are the small triangular 'corners' that help secure the sides of the hull to the deck. In modern fibreglass craft they are less obvious and may be incorporated into heavy hull-deck bonding, but in older yachts they are very obvious, often made from aesthetically shaped timbers. Bulkheads are the most widely used and efficient fittings for retaining the tube shape of the hull against wracking stresses. Apart from creating compartments, which make living in the hull more convenient, bulkheads provide enormous stiffening power, holding the hull in shape no matter how the seas twist and turn (or wrack) it.

The stresses of wracking are potentially the most damaging of all to the hull and, as mentioned before, in practice, most structural members come into play

when the boat is experiencing this type of movement. The deck beams prevent the hull from collapsing inwards and the stringers and keel act as a
spinal reinforcement. Together with the bulkheads
and knees they spread the stresses across the entire
structure of the hull, thus avoiding 'hot' spots
which may create a weakness and give way when
under excess load.

The corkscrewing effect of running before a
big sea creates the greatest wracking stresses. Then,
like the shoebox, the hull is being twisted one way
as a wave lifts under the stern, while the bow,
driving down into the trough, is forced hard the
other way. As the wave passes under the boat the
position is reversed, and the boat is twisted the
other way, with her bow now in the crest and the
stern in the trough, trying to swing round and meet
the following wave as it moves in. This dramatic

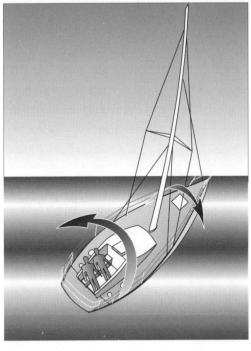

and violent action really tests every part of a hull's construction and if there is a
weakness, it is under these conditions that it is most likely to show up.

While the hull is going through its contortions in the seas, the mast is
meantime gyrating wildly across the sky, creating even more stresses. Unlike the

*The stresses of
wracking are
potentially the most
damaging of all to the
hull and, in practice,
most structural
members come into
play when the boat is
experiencing this type
of movement.*

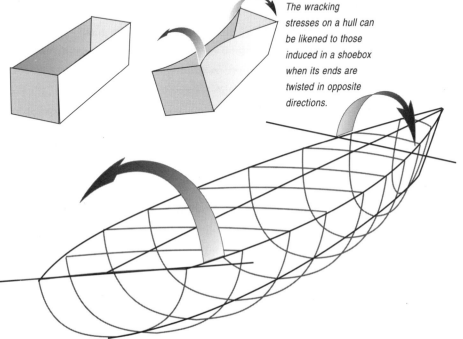

*The wracking
stresses on a hull can
be likened to those
induced in a shoebox
when its ends are
twisted in opposite
directions.*

heavy, but even, stresses experienced when sailing hard on the wind or even reaching, the stresses created by running before a quartering sea are uneven and very vicious.

The mast literally whips from side to side as the boat goes through the corkscrewing motion, transferring enormous strains through the rigging first to one side of the hull then the other. Although the stress will be predominantly on the windward side, so severe is the motion of the boat in this situation that surprisingly heavy loads will be placed on the leeward structures too.

While running before the seas is a popular method of riding out a blow with many experienced skippers, it can only be carried out with any degree of peace of mind if the hull is totally sound and seaworthy. While other conditions can also test a hull to its limits, the wracking stresses of running before a big sea are the most likely to create problems and show up any weaknesses in the hull's construction.

Running before is also one of the most stressful conditions for crew since at no stage can the boat be left to her own devices, as is the case when lying to a sea anchor or lying ahull. Considering all these factors, it is quite surprising, really, that running before a sea is such a popular method of riding out a blow with experienced salts.

A wave breaking underneath the boat creates turbulent water that will reduce the efficiency of the rudder

Broaching

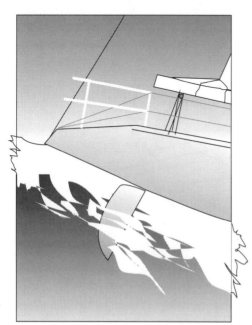

This is a condition which can create very damaging stresses to a hull, and for that reason must be avoided if at all possible. There are a number of forms of broaching, the more correctly named being when the boat gets out of control either as a result of a savage wind gust or a rogue sea, and slews across the wave, often rounding up into the wind or falling off the wave. This brings a whole Pandora's Box of stresses to bear on the hull: wracking, severe heeling, pounding, to mention but a few.

Hence, it is a good idea to avoid broaching where possible.

It is also the sort of condition that brings big seas aboard with the risk of hatches, doors or windows being stove in, and plays havoc with below-deck gear as the boat is often flattened on her ear, followed by a violent

Either as a result of a savage wind gust or a rogue sea, the boat slews across the wave, often rounding up into the wind or being rolled by a wave .

return to the upright. Of course, it cannot always be avoided, particularly in extreme sea and wind conditions. Generally, it is the result of overcanvassing and it is a wise skipper who reduces sail before the onset of a blow, thus reducing the risk of broaching and also the need to send crew up on deck to reef sails under extreme conditions.

Falling off a wave

This can be part of a broaching mishap or it can occur in the course of normal heavy-weather sailing. It is particularly likely to occur when the boat is driving hard on the wind into a big sea. If wind and sea are running in the same direction,

The most common form of falling off a wave is when the wave moves rapidly from beneath the boat, leaving her poised in space.

as is usually the case, then a boat driving ahead close-hauled will be taking the seas at an angle to the bow. This is normally a comfortable and safe way of sailing providing the seas don't start to get too big. In deep ocean waters, even big seas are relatively safe since they may not become particularly steep, but in shallower regions and notably when closing on a coastline, the seas will tend to rear up and develop a 'wall' or face over which the crest will break.

At this point the danger of 'falling off' starts to become a real possibility. As the boat drives up through the crest, the wave moves rapidly beneath her, leaving her literally poised, hanging in space. The wave continues to move and the boat falls into the oncoming trough with a bone-jarring crunch that does nothing for the crew's physical well-being, and even less for the structure of the hull.

As a rule she comes down on one side, having been heeled over close-hauled, and the greatest impact is on the hull skin along the bow to about midships. This will test fibreglass skins in particular as they generally have far less bracing behind them than timber hull skins. It is not unknown for such an impact to split the hull open, a terminal condition in the middle of storm. Other strains such as those from the severe whipping of the mast when the hull falls into the trough, can also create damaging stresses on parts of the hull.

There are other conditions which can cause the boat to fall off a wave, such as when she is sailing parallel to the line of the waves. Much depends on the shape of the seas and the speed the boat is crossing them. Once the seas build to the point of developing steep faces it is generally time to look at taking off more sail and reducing speed, or even adopting one of the methods of riding it out. There is little to be gained in driving the boat hard through a steep sea unless she is racing, and then, of course, the consequences are an acceptable risk. But steep waves, even if the boat is not falling off them, create extreme discomfort for everyone on board and put unnecessary strains on the hull.

Other stresses and strains

There are, of course, many other stresses and strains which affect a hull when working in a seaway. Some relate directly to the actions of the sea, some to the actions of the wind. They are far too numerous to list in detail here and far to numerous for the average boat-owner to be concerned about. Only the boat's designer needs to be aware of them and make the necessary adjustments to the structure of the boat so that their effect is minimised.

The upward pull on the shrouds when the mast and sails are under full load is typical of this type of stress, and correctly seated chainplates are the mechanism used to distribute the strains. The whipping of the mast when the hull is plunging in and out of seas, and its ferocious gyrations when the boat is lying ahull add even more to the load on the rigging and thus the chainplates.

Even in a moderate blow, enormous stresses will be placed on these parts. Suffice it to say that a well-designed and well-built yacht will be capable of coping with them in any kind of weather.

CHAPTER 2

A Sound Hull

A boat is only as good as its skipper, they say, but the reverse also applies. For no matter how skilled and experienced the skipper, if the boat is not sound and seaworthy, she will founder. If the hull cannot keep the sea on the outside, it is usually only a matter of time before human endeavour, the pumps and the bucket brigade fail and the water makes inroads. And that may mean the end of the line for both boat and crew.

Of course, this applies on all waters, whether close inshore or halfway across an ocean and applies to all boats, whether power or sail. But at least in coastal waters there is a often back-up in the form of emergency services which, while they may not save the boat, can save the crew. Over the horizon and far out at sea, hundreds, perhaps even thousands of miles from any emergency services, both boat and crew are on their own.

That's when all the chickens come home to roost and all the things you meant to fix in the quiet of the marina now loom as vitally important, perhaps even the key to survival. The heavier gauge stays you intended to fit before you ran out of money. The port or window scuttles that were to be fixed, but you just ran out of time. The rudder fitting that had been loose for a while, but seemed to be OK just before you left port. The bilges which you meant to clean but which never got crossed off the list. Now, with the wind at gale force and the seas building to miniature Mount Everests, these things will come back to haunt you.

A sound and seaworthy boat is, arguably, better insurance even than the finest crew with the best boat-handling skills and experience, for a boat can, and often has, survived on its own through the worst onslaught. Indeed, this was a lesson learned from the disastrous Fastnet Race of 1979, when a number of abandoned craft were picked up after the gale, having survived the brunt of the storm with no one on board.

Experienced ocean travellers will, when the chips are down, often leave the boat to its own devices, battening themselves firmly below decks and allowing the boat to ride out the blow on its own. Providing the boat is sound and seaworthy this is a recognised and safe procedure. The emphasis being, of course, on the fact that the boat is sound and seaworthy.

A not uncommon experience when crossing the Southern Ocean, running

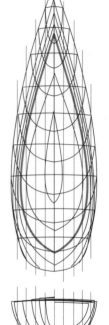

The obvious starting place for a sound boat is with the design of the hull itself.

25

A not uncommon experience when crossing the Southern Ocean, running before the giant swells that inhabit that region, is to pitch-pole, or end-for-end. The boat, running down the face of a giant sea, digs in her bow. The impetus of the wave coming up astern, lifts her stern and rolls her over in a forward direction.

before the giant swells that inhabit that region, is to pitch-pole, or end-for-end. The boat, running down the face of a giant sea, digs in her bow. The impetus of the wave coming up astern, lifts her stern and rolls her over in a forward direction, literally base over apex!

Almost certainly this means the loss of mast and rig, but if the boat is sound and well-battened down, and the hull is not damaged in the process, there is every chance she will come upright, leaving only a messy deckhead to indicate she has turned a full 360 degrees! This has happened to a number of yachts, some handled by well-known and very professional skippers. All have survived with nothing worse than extreme discomfort, a few hours of repair work and scars on the deckhead.

Certainly, in most cases these skippers were experienced, and certainly their experience and skill had much to do with preparing the boat for such an eventuality. But when it came to the crunch, it was the boat that was the survival factor, the crew just hung on for dear life. The experience and skill of the skipper showed most in his selection of a sound and seaworthy hull, for without this, there would have been little to hang on to!

Lying ahull in a big seaway is another case in point. Once again, the skill and experience of the skipper lies in selecting the right hull to withstand the enormous wracking stresses that are placed on the hull in this situation. This is a favoured method of riding out a blow in the open ocean, and generally speaking it is a practical, albeit uncomfortable method. But its success does depend entirely on the soundness of the hull, for in this configuration, tortured by the seas to a point beyond anything planned by her designer, the boat must withstand exceptional stresses and strains akin to, if not worse than, those experienced in pitch-poling.

So what is a sound and seaworthy boat? What factors make an ordinary yacht capable of withstanding these huge strains that are rarely experienced in normal sailing?

What gives her the ability to ride out even the most torturous sea conditions yet not only remain in one piece, but also avoid any serious damage to her hull structure?

A seaworthy structure

The obvious starting place is with the design of the hull itself. In today's modern yacht-racing world, where speed is king and lightness of weight a vital factor, there is a tendency to forget some of the basic principles of a structurally sound hull when the first images are laid down on the drawing board.

In recent years, a number of yachts in the Sydney-Hobart yacht race-consistently the toughest of all the blue-water classics-have retired with damage that related directly to lightweight construction. In terms of sails and deck gear, this is to be expected, of course; fast boats trying to go faster are always candidates for a washing-line of torn Kevlar by the time they cross the finish line. But the sails are in an area where economy of weight is an acceptable means of gaining speed, for there is little danger to life and limb in blowing out sails. While it may create unwelcome stresses on an owner's pocket, the old adage attributed to one of the most famous of all racing yacht owners, Sir Thomas Lipton, holds good: if you are concerned about the cost, you can't afford it!

Small boats using close inshore waters are at least within reach of assistance if something goes wrong. In the middle of an ocean there is little help available.

Similarly, sheets and spars that carry away are an acceptable part of riding out a seaway if you are pushing the boat to her limit. But it begins to get more serious when masts come down, and it can take on terminal proportions if the hull is damaged. Even in yacht racing, safety measures are supposed to avoid this type of occurrence, but the events in the Sydney-Hobart described earlier indicate that sacrifices in hull structure are being made in the name of speed. This is not on, even for ocean racing, and it is definitely not on when you are out there on your own.

Why the difference? Because ocean racing is generally carefully monitored and a yacht which suffers serious damage during a race is usually able to obtain help quickly and efficiently. By contrast, an ocean-cruising yacht, travelling alone across the vast open spaces, can be easily beyond any kind of assistance. Even if her distress call is picked up, and a rescue attempt launched, the distances involved may make it impossible to reach her other than by ship, a process that can take many days.

This is not to condone the use of less structurally sound vessels in ocean racing; far from it. Any vessel which puts to sea for any purpose whatsoever should be structurally sound. But it is important to highlight the greater danger of a lone yacht suffering serious hull damage in the desolate, isolated regions of the world's oceans, as compared to the closely monitored participants in an offshore race.

Basic features

Whether prominent or not, whether visible or not, there are certain structural members which are common to all boats, no matter what design they follow or what material they are constructed from. These are the vitally important members that will determine how well a vessel stands up in a seaway, and how safe and

sound the hull will be. They create the basic skeleton of a seaworthy vessel which is common to all seagoing craft, from small pleasure boats to ocean-going liners.

Main members

The hull of any seagoing vessel, large or small, is formed around a basic structure in just the same way that a shore-side building has a reinforced structure around which the shell is erected. Naturally, different methods of design and different types of building materials call for different structural fabrication. Timber and steel boats, for example, have very prominent structural features in the hull, consisting of longitudinal and transverse members of different sizes and gauges. These are fabricated into a framework around which the skin of the hull is wrapped.

Concrete boats have similar fabrications, although much of the strength in this type of construction comes from the wire or steel mesh integrated throughout the cement plaster skin, and many of the structural members so prominent in timber or metal craft are less obvious. Fibreglass yachts also follow this trend, with the glass fibres integrated throughout the resin skin reinforcing the structural strength of the boat and reducing the need for many of the less prominent members.

Keel

This is the backbone of the hull, and like the backbone of anything, living or manufactured, it is the most important structural feature. Without a backbone,

Homo sapiens would have to walk on all fours, aircraft would add a new dimension to the term 'belly landing' and major building structures would waft and bend in even the lightest of summer breezes.

The keel of a yacht is sometimes incorrectly described as the 'downward projecting bit' below the waterline. While this is also known as the keel, it is not the structural keel, being concerned mainly with lateral resistance to the water. In terms of structural strength, the keel is the strong structural member that runs along the centreline of the bottom of the boat from stem-post to stern-post. In timber vessels it is a heavy, solid beam, in steel and concrete craft a girder, and in fibreglass construction it is usually fabricated either by encasing some other material or fabricating the structural member from the fibreglass material itself.

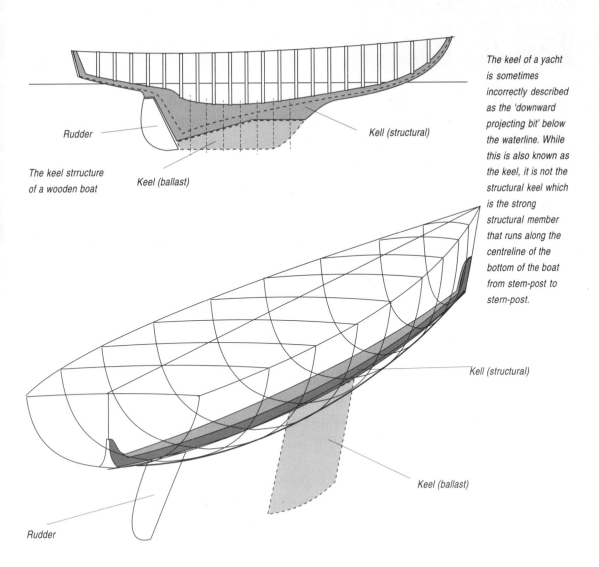

Rudder

Kell (structural)

The keel strructure
of a wooden boat

Keel (ballast)

Kell (structural)

Keel (ballast)

Rudder

The keel of a yacht is sometimes incorrectly described as the 'downward projecting bit' below the waterline. While this is also known as the keel, it is not the structural keel which is the strong structural member that runs along the centreline of the bottom of the boat from stem-post to stern-post.

31

Ballast is a key factor in the stability of a seagoing yacht. In most vessels designed for open sea work, ballast weighing 30% - 40% of the total weight is necessary.

Carbon fibre may be used where maximum strength and least weight are required.

Whatever the composition of the keel structure, the important factor is that it runs the length of the vessel from bow to stern, along the centreline, and is strong enough to resist longitudinal bending. The types of stresses that are imposed on a boat when working in a seaway and which create such bending forces are described in Chapter 1. The keel is involved in countering most of these.

Beam shelf

This is also called the deck strake or sheer strake. It is the deck's counterpart to the keel, but instead of running along the centreline of the boat, it is divided and runs along each side at deck level. This is to enable deck openings such as hatches and skylights to be located on the centreline without the need to cut the beam shelf, thus weakening it.

The beam shelf is constructed in much the same way as the keel, although it is usually of lighter gauge as there are two of these members as opposed to one keel. Also, unlike the keel, they are not straight, but curve to follow the shape of the deck plan and sheer of the hull. However, the structural requirements of the beam shelf are similar to those of the keel in that it must prevent longitudinal bending of the hull when the boat is being tossed around in a seaway.

The beam shelf serves a number of other purposes. It joins the deck to the sides of the hull and provides a platform onto which cross members-beams-can be landed. This accounts for its description as the 'beam shelf'. Because it runs the full length of the hull, it needs to be a very rigid structure and capable of withstanding considerable stresses. Large ocean-going ships which have broken up in a seaway usually owe their demise to the failure of this structural member-known as a 'sheer strake' in big-ship circles.

Beams

While the longitudinal strength of the boat is dependent on the keel and beam shelves, the transverse stresses are countered by cross-members. The hull is not unlike a box in cross-section, and a box can easily be crushed if it is not rigidly constructed-sending a box through the mail will prove this! To prevent this

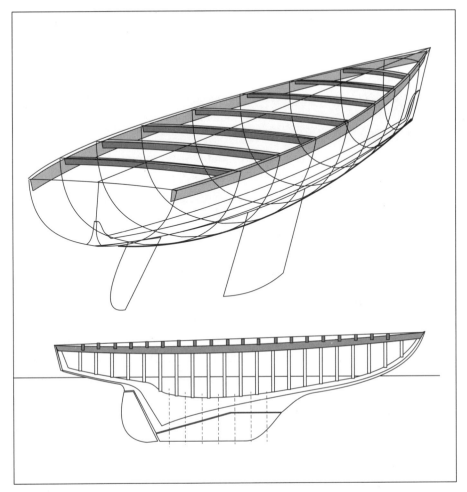

To prevent topsides crushing and the deck sagging, the hull is fitted with beams which run beneath the deck from one side to another. In the case of older style timber boats, beams are placed at frequent intervals along the length of the hull.

crushing effect, the hull is fitted with beams which run beneath the deck from one side to another and are secured to the side of the hull, usually onto the beam shelf.

Beams can be fitted at frequent intervals along the length of the hull, as is the case with older style timber and steel boats, or staggered at locations where they complement bulkheads or provide strength at high-stress points. One such area is the the point where the mast is stepped on deck. To provide the required support beneath the mast and transfer its stresses to other parts of the hull, deck beams are often used.

Another use for these beams, of course, is to provide a platform onto which the deck is laid. In modern fibreglass yachts the beams and deck are often moulded together as a single unit and the whole bonded to the sides of the hull by way of the beam shelf. But where a separate deck is fitted, beams are used as the landing for whatever type of deck is used. Beams are usually cambered, both to give added strength and to slope the deck to allow water to run off.

Added support to areas of weakness, such as the deck cutouts for hatches and skylights, is another use for beams. Indeed, it could be said that wherever additional strength or support is required at deck level, a beam is likely to be used to do the job. Any weakness is then spread across the hull instead of being localised and creating a 'hot spot' which can fail under the stresses of riding out a sea.

Bulkheads

The 'box' or 'tube' section formed by the hull is, as already described, very vulnerable to 'crushing'. In addition, wracking stresses, caused by the box shape being pushed to one side or another, can cause eventual collapse.

To a certain degree these stresses are countered by the deck beams running from side to side, and in older timber and steel boats by 'ribs' or 'timbers' which run down this inside of the hull, holding the skin in place and preventing it from collapsing inwards. 'Knees'-triangular pieces fitted between the deck and the side of the hull around the beam shelf-are another means of countering transverse stresses.

Modern fibreglass craft tend to utilise the structural strength of the glass fibres reinforcing the resin body of the material to create much of the hull strength, so ribs and knees are less often seen in hulls built of this material.

Despite all these structural members, however, there is still considerable

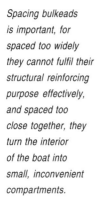

Spacing bulkeads is important, for spaced too widely they cannot fulfil their structural reinforcing purpose effectively, and spaced too close together, they turn the interior of the boat into small, inconvenient compartments.

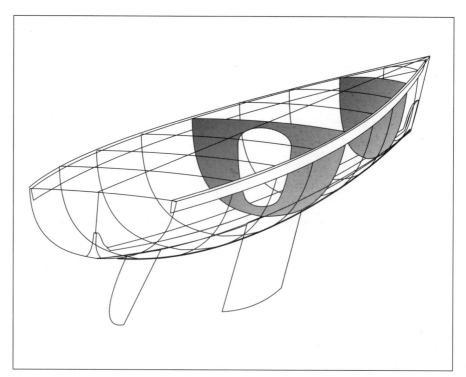

risk of the box structure becoming damaged by wracking or crushing stresses. To prevent this, bulkheads are placed at intervals along the inside of the hull and these provide the major structural strength of the box section.

Bulkheads are built to exactly fit the interior shape of the hull so that not only is the hull skin held firm against any outside pressures, but the whole box shape is rigidly held from wracking or any other transverse movement. It goes without saying that these are some of the most significant of all structural members in the hull make-up.

Bulkheads are, however, rather inconvenient as they break the interior of the hull into sections. Spacing is important, for spaced too widely they cannot fulfil their structural reinforcing purpose effectively, and spaced too close together, they turn the interior of the boat into a rabbit warren. It is up to the designer to reach a compromise in this problem, allowing spaces between bulkhead large enough to make comfortable living areas, yet not sufficiently large to weaken the hull.

Hull skin

This is the medium that keeps the water on the outside of the hull, so if a boat is to be sound and seaworthy, it must have a well-constructed and waterproof skin. Timber and steel are less used now, and concrete is not over-popular. The most

A seaworthy hull slips easily through the water, keeping the sea on the outside where it is supposed to be!

effective material of recent years is fibreglass in which layers of glass fibres are impregnated with a hard-setting resin to form a reinforced, relatively thin layer which is very strong and resistant to most maritime problems.

Fibreglass hulls are generally moulded in one piece with most, if not all the structural members integrated into the moulding. Another moulding, similarly reinforced, includes the deck and cabin structure, and when bonded together these two create a vessel that is structurally complete.

Not all hull forms are simply moulded from fibreglass. There are a number of different methods of using the modern material. A composite of fibreglass and some other material (balsa is one) in a 'sandwich' structure is strong and much lighter than a full fibreglass lay-up. With carbon fibres and other modern synthetic strengtheners, boatbuilders can achieve light weight for racing and other specific requirements that might be called for according to the planned use of the yacht.

With racing craft, cost is usually no object and therefore expensive lightweight construction methods, such as the use of carbon fibres, can be used if the boat is intended to be a crack racer. A cruising owner, looking for economy rather than speed, will probably opt for a construction that will be strong, albeit fairly heavy, but much cheaper that the lightweight flyer material.

As with everything, boats can come in all forms and constructions and can be built from a number of different materials. But whatever the construction, the

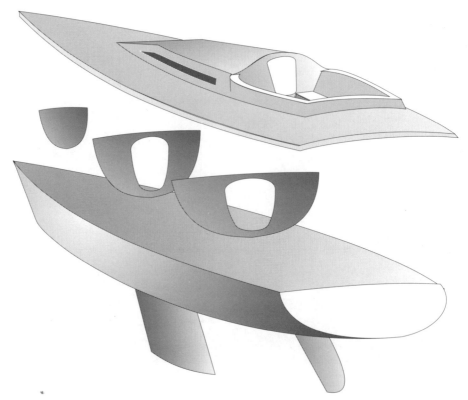

Fibreglass hulls are generally moulded in one piece with most, if not all the structural members integrated into the moulding. Another moulding incorporates the deck and cabin structure. These two create a vessel that is structurally complete.

basic structural requirements must be followed or the boat, whether racing or cruising, will not stand up to the sea.

Timber hull skins come in a number of forms, ranging from straight planking, through laminated layers to hot moulded or even more sophisticated lay-up systems. Older boats will mostly either have clinker or carvel planking. The former is an overlapping system of laying planks on the structural framework, in the latter the planks are laid flush. In terms of strength there is probably little to choose between a well-constructed skin of any material, but one weakness of timber planking is the likelihood of leaking through the seams between the planks as the boat ages or works in a seaway.

This is rarely a serious problem in normal use, as the seams open gradually and can easily be caulked by slipping or careening the boat. In the open ocean, however, this can be more disconcerting, especially if the boat is riding out a blow, as it is hard to caulk from the inside. Once the seams begin to work, unless they are caulked quickly, the boat will start to take on dangerous amounts of water.

This can also be a problem with timber decks, especially laid decks where again the seams between the planks can open up and leak. Since timber shrinks when it is dried, the action of a hot sun can soon open up seams between laid planks of the deck, allowing water down below. This is not as serious a problem as with hull seams opening, since only a trickle of water will make its way through the decks, and these can soon be caulked. There is certainly no danger of the boat foundering. However, any water below decks is a problem, and even a trickle can put a radio or some other electrical gear out of action.

Steel and concrete boats are basically similar to fibreglass in that the homogeneous skin is unlikely to leak or open as a result of movement of the hull in a seaway and the leaking problems of a planked boat should not be experienced. If a steel hull opens up along a weld or a concrete hull cracks when riding out a blow, the situation is very serious indeed. About the only option left is prayer!

Hull openings

Providing the hull is soundly constructed, a yacht or motor yacht should be able to ride out any ocean weather except, perhaps, extremes such as tropical revolving storms (typhoons, hurricanes, cyclones) where even giant ocean ships can get into trouble. There are, however, weak areas in every hull that make even the strongest boat vulnerable in a seaway. These are the hull openings such as hatches, doorways, windows and skin fittings which create a vulnerable break in the otherwise sound 'tube' structure of the hull.

Big windows are an asset when cruising in sheltered waters, but can create severe problems in a seaway, where a window stove in by a sea can create terminal conditions for the boat.

Without these openings, survival in even the most savage blow would be far easier and certain, except perhaps in motor yachts where the risk of capsize is always present. But a keel yacht without hull openings would theoretically ride out even a cyclone, for as long as the hull remains intact no water can get inside and if no water can get inside, the boat can't sink!

Doors, hatches, windows

Hull openings are unfortunately essential in any craft to provide access for crew and to allow daylight, ventilation and engine cooling water into the interior of the hull. But unless these are correctly secured and made an integral part of the hull when riding out a storm, they create a weakness that can, and sometimes does, create an extremely dangerous situation.

Weaknesses caused by cutting into or removing parts of the hull structure for hatches, windows and the like are usually compensated for in the design and structure of the boat. But often the actual hatch, window or skin fitting used can cause problems by allowing access of water into the hull. In this way any deck opening for any purpose can destroy the watertight form of the hull and must be treated as a potential weak spot.

Many boat-owners are not aware of the ferocity of the sea in gale conditions and the enormous impact of a wave boarding the boat or crashing into the hull.

As a result, hatches, doors and windows which would seem more than adequate in normal conditions, can prove a weak link when the moment of truth arrives.

Big windows and doors are undesirable for a boat that is intended for ocean crossing. While it is possible to board them up and reduce the risks when a blow comes down, this is a temporary and often unsatisfactory procedure. The boards can be swept away or smashed by a single wave, thus leaving the deck opening vulnerable to the next big sea that comes aboard. Small windows and hatches are less vulnerable, and if they are stove in, the amount of water that can enter the hull is less likely to cause problems, or can be removed fairly quickly. Doors, such as those on big motor yachts, always create a major weakness and boarding them up is rarely sufficient to withstand the impact of a large sea coming over the side.

Skin fittings

Other hull openings exist where air or water is allowed into the boat. Ventilators are often designed to remain open even under adverse conditions so that air can be drawn into and exhausted out of the hull interior. These deck fittings allow air in but keep water out, although in a big seaway they may be overcome by the amount of water flooding the deck, and allow some to enter. However, as in the case of deck leaks, small amounts of water are not usually terminal although they can damage electrical equipment, and many experienced sailors seal off their ventilators before the onset of a blow.

The sailor's safety valve! Sea cocks should be fitted to every hull opening in seagoing craft.

Of considerably greater importance are the hull openings for engine, toilet and other discharges and inlets. Apart from creating the same sort of weakness as a window or hatch-albeit on a smaller scale-these fittings are below the waterline and therefore very vulnerable to damage. Indeed, damage to such openings can create problems even when the boat is lying to a mooring, and great care is necessary to see that they are maintained in good condition, fitted with efficient sea-cocks and, if damaged, immediately sealed off or repaired. The damage may not even be associated directly with the skin opening-a ruptured hose leading from a skin fitting can flood the boat if it is not immediately sealed off.

A good sea-cock close to the opening is the first essential to avoid such problems, so that any internal damage to the system can be sealed off at the skin.

Damage to the fitting itself may required the use of bungs or some other damage control equipment. It is not unknown for the skin fitting to be ripped bodily out of the skin leaving a sizeable hole beneath the waterline. Only a good sized bung hammered firmly home can fix this, so an extensive collection of bungs is an important part of any boat's emergency equipment.

A classic case of the dangers that can arise from underwater skin fittings occurred in the South Pacific, when a small cruising yacht, after an extensive passage around the islands was returning to its home base in New Zealand. For some reason known only to itself, the propeller shaft disconnected itself from the motor flange and slid quietly out of the stern gland and sank, leaving water pouring in through a hole of around 50 millimetres in diameter.

This should not be a terminal situation under normal conditions, but the single-handed skipper had omitted to put bungs aboard and he was unable to stem the flow. This seemingly small oversight brought his pleasant cruise to an untimely end. He was plucked from the sea by a rescue helicopter as his yacht sank beneath his feet. And all this in virtually calm weather.

CHAPTER 3

Buying a seagoing boat

It goes without saying that if a boat is to be sound and seaworthy and capable of withstanding anything the sea can throw at it, then its construction must incorporate all the structural features described in the previous chapters. Appearance is one thing, and naturally everyone likes to own a good-looking craft. Comfort is another, and while it is never really comfortable in any boat when the sea is blowing up into gale conditions, at least the basic necessities of comfort should be in place.

But the bottom line, regardless of appearance or comfort, is seaworthiness, for if the boat is not seaworthy then there is not much point in it being comfortable or attractive, since it will not survive for people to admire its nice lines or its luxury fittings. If you are planning an offshore passage, be it a coastal hop or an ocean crossing, the factors to look for in choosing the boat are those which affect safety and seaworthiness.

The main structural parts have been described already, and obviously these must come in for very close scrutiny when considering a purchase. But there are many more, smaller items which in themselves may not play a major part in making the boat seaworthy, but nevertheless can indirectly affect the boat's structure and her ability to ride out a big sea. The design of the boat and her 'seakindliness' have been discussed before, so before hauling a prospective buy out of the water for a full inspection, you should have decided if she has the right beam for length, the right entry, suitable cockpit, etc.

Now, with the boat up on the slipway, it is time to get down to the nitty-gritty. Is she really the boat for your planned voyage? The following is a rather generalised check list on what to look for on your out-of-water inspection.

Hull shapes

As with any vehicle used for any purpose, shape is an important factor in performance. Sleek, aerodynamic shapes are used to reduce drag and enhance

Modern fin keels (closest yacht) permit more manoeuverability, but do not offer the directional stability in a seaway of the traditional long keel (middle yacht). Bilge keels are great for landing on the hard, but are not greatly favoured for open sea work.

speed, whether it be in cars, aircraft or boats. Conversely, rugged, solid shapes tend to go with endurance and stamina rather than speed, and hulls designed to withstand the rigours of ocean crossings are more likely to be of solid, workman-like appearance than the sleek, lightweight hulls of racing craft.

Appearance is usually allied to construction where boats are concerned, and the lightweight flyers that whip around the buoys during a weekend race are usually of much less solid build than ocean 'wallopers'. That is not to say, of course, that cruising boats may not be as attractively designed as racers; many are every bit as aesthetically pleasing as the 'fast' boats. But, vessels not used for racing can afford to provide more space inside the hull and thus more comfortable accommodation, bigger and more powerful motors, and a generally more robust construction, all of which add up to a generally bigger and bulkier appearance.

The underwater shape of the hull is important, and here again there is a distinct difference between boats designed for racing and those where speed is not the ultimate aim. Boats intended to race, particularly round short courses, need to be very manoeuvrable. Swinging quickly from tack to tack when beating, or slipping smartly around a turning buoy, can be severely inhibited by a long keel.

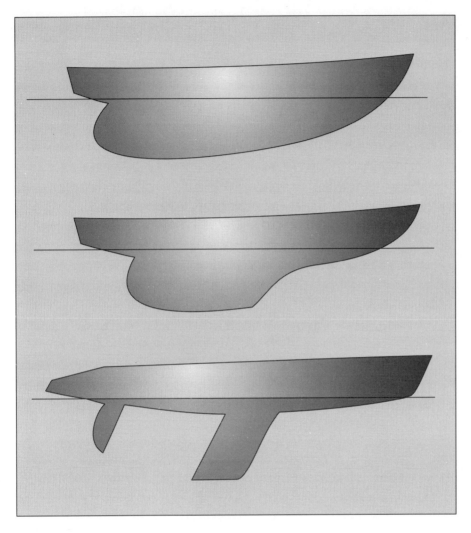

The long keel, with its ability to provide good directional stability, is ideal for ocean going, particularly when running before a big sea. The long line of the keel holds the boat steady. This reduces the need for much helm correction. Boats intended to race need to be very manoeuvrable. Swinging quickly from tack to tack when beating can be severely inhibited by a long keel, so this type of craft usually has a short fin keel.

The long, traditional keel creates considerable water resistance and slows the turn markedly. A short fin keel enables the boat to pivot around the centre of lateral resistance very quickly.

The reverse of this particular coin is that the long keel, with its ability to provide good directional stability, is ideal for ocean going, particularly when running before a big sea. The long line of the keel holds the boat steady and resists the attempts of the waves to push her off course. This reduces the need for much helm correction. This is quite a different proposition to the action of a hull fitted with a fin keel where the directional stability is lost and the only control is from the rudder. In this case, the helm is being used constantly to correct wild swings; a tiring activity for the helmsman and a wearing process for the steering gear. So where ocean going is the main intention, a boat with a long keel is preferable.

Monohull or multihull

The different type of hull forms are also worthy of consideration, although this is a controversial area and there are many schools of thought on the subject. Dedicated multihull sailors will decry any attempt to claim that their style of hull form is not as seaworthy as the traditional monohull, and in some situations, they are probably correct. Without wishing to use these pages to fuel the controversy, it is important that the basic factors affecting a boat's performance in a seaway be examined before a choice is made as to which of the hull forms is going to carry you safely through the storms and vagaries of an ocean passage.

As mentioned in a number of places in this book, the traditional monohull, providing it is soundly constructed, has at least 35 per cent ballast ratio and, if properly handled, is virtually indestructible in normal ocean-crossing conditions. It is designed to ride out even severe storm and sea conditions and if capsized, is totally self-righting.

Their wide beam gives catamaran hulls great stability in sheltered waters, but they can be subject to other problems in a big seaway.

While a well-constructed multihull will also meet most of these requirements, it does not meet them all. If capsized, a multihull cannot usually be righted, and the possibility of a capsize is always present due to the nature of the hull shape. Twin or triple hulls create a broad beam in relation to length and while, generally, a wide beam tends to inhibit capsize, this theory works only in relatively flat

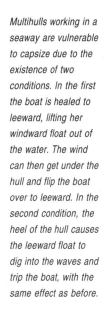

Multihulls working in a seaway are vulnerable to capsize due to the existence of two conditions. In the first the boat is healed to leeward, lifting her windward float out of the water. The wind can then get under the hull and flip the boat over to leeward. In the second condition, the heel of the hull causes the leeward float to dig into the waves and trip the boat, with the same effect as before.

water. In a big seaway, the well-spaced hulls span a wide expanse of sea, which render the boat very vulnerable to waves moving in and under it, particularly when these waves approach from the beam or the quarter.

There are two major situations which can lead to a capsize under these conditions. In the first the boat is heeled to leeward under a moderate or strong blow, and is racing through the water with the leeward hull or float partially or wholly immersed. Normally this is no problem and the lee hull moves forward unimpeded through the water. But if a large, steep wave rolls down and buries this lee hull the weight of water will prevent it rising or continuing to move forward easily. The momentum of the boat and the pressure of the wind, then combine to

45

flip the boat over to leeward or perhaps break off the lee float. Either will result in a capsize.

The other situation that can cause problems for multihulls is again most likely when reaching across a beam sea. A big wave moving in from windward passes under the hull and in doing so, since the boat is heeled to leeward, lifts the windward float or hull clear of the water. The 'slope wind' that moves up the face of a wave and is used to provide the gliding action of albatrosses, gets beneath the windward hull and forces the hull even farther to leeward, eventually inducing the tripping action of the leeward float described earlier, and again capsizing the boat.

Of course, these are theoretical scenarios, but experience in seafaring and a study of recorded multihull accidents gives them good credence. Lacking the stability of a ballast keel, the multihull form must always be suspect for ocean work, and whether or not the advantages of this type of hull outweigh this rather dominant disadvantage, is a matter for the individual boat purchaser to determine.

Motor yacht hulls

In choosing a power vessel for offshore waters, a hull with a good power unit is the best insurance against getting caught out.

These are, in general, fairly vulnerable to storms at sea. Lacking the deep ballast keel of a conventional yacht they are liable to prove unstable in rough conditions and, with a sizeable sea on the beam, can be capsized with little likelihood of self-righting. Much depends on the design of the boat, of course, and some power

vessels are built to withstand a certain degree of heavy sea conditions in offshore waters. But most pleasure craft are intended for fishing or for comfortable relaxation in relatively sheltered waters and ability to ride out a storm in the ocean is not a prime consideration.

Most have sufficient power and operate in relatively inshore waters, so that at the onset of a storm, they can run for shelter before conditions deteriorate and access to a harbour or bay is too dangerous to attempt. Indeed, this is the factor which many power boat-owners see as the main safety feature of such craft: the hull is designed to run fast from trouble, not to ride out big seas.

In choosing a power vessel for offshore waters, then, a hull with a good power unit is the best insurance against getting caught out. A reasonably deep 'v' will offer more comfortable riding than a flat bottom and a good beam will provide some stability should the boat have to tackle heavy beam seas. Twin motors provide the comforting knowledge that if one motor fails, there is a back-up to take you home, and an extended fuel range can be useful if the closest harbour is not accessible and the nearest shelter is some distance away.

Wetted surfaces

This is the term given to those areas of the hull which are normally under water and which can only be examined when the boat is slipped. The antifouling needs to be scrubbed back hard because marine growth of any kind-even slime-can conceal skin faults. Indeed, one of the most insidious of all skin faults in fibreglass boats-osmosis-can be easily missed if the inspection is not very thorough.

Osmosis

This is basically the 'bubbling' of the gel coat (the outer skin surface) as a result of permeation of water beneath the skin. Poor quality gel coat or age are the main causes, so a check on who built the boat and when would be a good step to take before the inspection begins. When the underwater areas of the hull are permanently immersed, water sometimes permeates through the gel coat, creating pockets of water under the surface which, in turn, form bubbles or blisters on the outer skin.

These bubbles may be in small rashes, like a child's chickenpox infection, or can form large, undulating bumps which can sometimes be hard to see. The latter are more dangerous, but if there is a large area covered by rashes of small

47

blisters, these, too can lead to big problems. With the hull well scrubbed clean, a hose should be played across the surface. When thoroughly wetted and shining, undulations and bumps are much easier to spot. Running your hand across the surface will also help pick up smaller blisters which may be difficult to pick up by eye.

In the initial stages, osmosis in itself does not create a structural problem, but with time it will spread, and the water locked into the blisters or bubbles will invade the laid-up structure of the fibreglass, by means of capillary action along the glass fibres. Taken to its extreme, this could cause the structure of the glass fibre to disintegrate. And, of course, before that happens, it will weaken the structure so that it will become vulnerable under the stresses of riding out a sea.

Osmosis can be cured, generally by sanding off the gel coat and laying the blister cavities bare, then drying them out thoroughly. Epoxy filler is mostly used to fill the cavities when dry, and the repaired area sealed off with an epoxy paint. Providing it is applied in time, this treatment can totally cure the problem, but more often than not the repair job is an expensive one, and there is always the risk that the osmosis has not been totally removed.

Concrete cancer

This is a similar situation to osmosis, but restricted to concrete hulls. The lay-up of a concrete hull uses steel netting as a reinforcement and cement plaster as the bonding material instead of the glass reinforcement and resin of fibreglass construction. Providing the water is kept totally outside the hull skin, there should be no problem, but if water permeates a poor plaster finish or, more likely, if the skin is damaged, and water comes into contact with the steel mesh, rust will set in. Particularly is this the case with sea water which is a major catalyst in causing steel to rust.

Just as the water can move through the glass fibre lay-up by capillary action along the glass fibres, so the rust eats its way along the steel mesh like an insidious worm quietly chomping away out of sight, but creating severe structural damage. Again, the worst scenario is the total collapse of the hull skin structure, but long before that areas of weakness will develop where there is no reinforcing to withstand the stresses of the hull moving in a seaway, and it will just break up.

There is no cure for concrete cancer, and as already mentioned, it is very hard to detect. Small rust 'weeps' on the outside (or inside) of the hull skin are often the only indication. Any signs of rust anywhere on the surface of a concrete hull should be treated with great suspicion.

Electrolytic corrosion

Concrete cancer is one of the most insidious of all forms of hull deterioration. It is, of course, limited to concrete vessels.

This is the underwater 'hoodoo' of steel vessels. In its most common form it appears as rust, but it can work more insidiously in areas where it may not be expected-notably around fittings, propellers, rudders, etc. It comes about as the result of galvanic action between two dissimilar metals in which one survives and one is literally eaten away. Steel is an alloy of different metals, so the galvanic action which creates rust is the result of one metal in the alloy reacting against another. The weaker of the two is eaten away, leaving the familiar pitting that is found beneath any rusty surface.

Rust is easily spotted and just as easily treated, even in underwater areas. Galvanic action affecting other metals in the underwater areas can be inhibited by fitting sacrificial anodes to the hull. These are zinc plates or blocks which 'attract' the galvanic action away from other metal parts of the hull or fittings. The sacrificial anodes are eaten away and need to be replaced every so often. This process prevents the galvanic action from affecting other metals. The placement, size and composition of the sacrificial anodes varies from boat to boat, but the out-of-water inspection will reveal their condition and the possible need for replacement.

Metal to be protected	Safe combination	Avoid
Copper, Brasses Bronzes	Copper Brasses Bronzes Monel Metal Stainless Steel	Aluminium Galvanised Iron Galvanised Steel Zinc
Stainless Steel	Copper Brasses Aluminiun Alloys Monel Metal	Galvanised Iron Gavinised Steel
Aluminium Alloys	Stainless Steel Galvanised Iron Galvanised Steel Cadmium Plated Steel	Copper Brasses Bronzes Lead

Electrolytic action, which creates the problem, is not confined to steel boats, although the steel hull structure naturally makes this type of vessel most vulnerable. Most vessels have metal fittings beneath the waterline-notably propellers which are extremely vulnerable as they are often made from bronze-and should be fitted with sacrificial anodes to control galvanic activity below the waterline.

Galvanic action can also be inhibited by separating the two metals with an insulating material. Galvanic action requires the two metals to be in physical contact or the corrosive current cannot flow. Above deck fittings such as a bronze fitting on an aluminium mast can be insulated by a mica pad (or some similar insulator) placed between the two metals. However, beneath the waterline it is impossible to stop the flow of current between two dissimilar metals because the sea water surrounding the hull creates the contact. Table 1 indicates the list of major susceptible metals and the degree in which they are affected by the electrolytic process.

Sacrificial anodes on a power boat hull reduce the effect of galvanic action on the propellers.

Rot and worm

Far from escaping the underwater problems of other types of hulls, timber vessels have more than their fair share. The most obvious is rot which, in the case of wetted surfaces, is invariably 'wet' rot. This is familiar to even non-nautical people, being the saturation of the wood fibres with resultant degeneration.

It is easily found, the simplest method being to tap the hull surfaces with a screwdriver. An area affected by rot will give a dull sound compared to the noise from sound timbers. Another method is to simply press the skin surfaces with your fingers; any sign of softness could indicate the presence of rot. It goes without saying that rot is potentially dangerous, even in small areas. The collapse of even a small section of one plank can allow access of water to the hull, and if the rot spreads, the hull will disintegrate.

A more insidious problem with underwater areas of timber boats is the marine or toredo worm. This is found mainly in warmer waters although a variety of worm is found in most sailing waters around the world. The worm burrows into the timber skin of the hull and promptly disappears, eating its way steadily through the timber, often without resurfacing. It achieves much the same result as concrete cancer, a seemingly wholesome surface, with nothing but a shell inside.

Marine worms vary in size, and often the only indication of their presence is a pinhole where they entered. Obviously, very careful inspection of the underwater areas is essential when the boat is slipped, for removing a severe infestation of worm will almost certainly mean replanking the affected part of the hull. Prevention is the key factor with this pest, and a hull that has been regularly and properly anti-fouled is unlikely to suffer worm problems. A hull which has been neglected and left in the water unattended or treated with cheap anti-fouling should be regarded with suspicion and given a very thorough examination on the slipway.

The topsides

Being very visible, the topsides should not require the detailed examination so essential with underwater areas. Most problems which can occur in this part of the hull are those already described, such as rust in the case of steel or concrete hulls and rot in timber skins, and these are fairly obvious in even a superficial examination. Loose fastenings in timber, or physical damage to fibreglass, timber or concrete are all fairly easy to spot and if they have been professionally repaired, should not be a problem in the future. Amateur repair work, of course, is usually obvious and is always suspect.

High topsides are important for deep-sea work if only to ensure that the boat is reasonably dry when the seas pick up. There is nothing inefficient about a 'submarine' type hull, as low-wooded boats are often called, and the chances are it will be as structurally sound and seaworthy as a high-wooded boat. But having the sea pouring across the decks, even if not endangering the boat, can create problems for a crew working on deck, and the general trend is to keep the water where it belongs wherever possible, and that means outside the boat.

The type of bow or stern is mainly dependent on the type of sailing planned. Offshore racing boats will have shapes that extract maximum advantage from the rules, but a cruising yacht that is not in a hurry and wants to enjoy a degree of comfort while on long passages will have a solid, perhaps even bulky look about her. Some experienced ocean sailors prefer canoe sterns, claiming that they provide more security and ease of handling with following seas. Certainly, boats with wide, flat stern areas invite pooping when a big sea is coming up astern. Most motor yachts fall into this category and are not usually good in a following sea.

On deck

Deck fittings can be important when the boat is in a seaway. Most are checked and possibly renewed before setting out on a passage. Safety rails are the major factor

in this area, and particularly on yachts, it is important to ensure that these totally enclose the deck and provide good protection for any crew working on deck. They must be well secured to withstand the weight of a body hurled against them, and the rails themselves should be of plastic-covered stainless steel wire of sufficient strength to take the weight of crewmen who are secured to them by safety harnesses.

A good hull shape, a clear deck and small windows make for a good ocean-going boat.

Another factor to look for on a deck inspection is the efficiency of ventilators. They must be capable of allowing good air into the cabin, which might need to be totally battened down in a blow, and yet prevent access of water. Similarly, windows, doors and hatches should be checked, bearing in mind the comments made on these fittings in Chapter 2. While using the hose to check the watertightness of all these items, the deck can also be given a thorough soaking to check for leaks. Particularly is this the case with timber boats and even more particularly with laid decks. Although rarely dangerous, leaking decks can create considerable discomfort for crew, to say nothing of putting electric and electronic equipment out of action.

Checking most of the deck gear is a question of finding out how well the boat is equipped, what conditions the gear is in and how much it will cost to bring the equipment and fittings up to seagoing standard.

Mast, spars and rigging

Few owners will be willing to allow the mast to be unstepped for a pre-sale inspection, although for a yacht that is intended for offshore work, particularly ocean crossing, the area above the deck is every bit as important as the wetted surfaces. Slipping the boat for inspection of the underwater areas is an accepted part of sale negotiations and there is a very strong case for lowering the mast. However, depending on the size and cost of the vessel, some individual negotiations might be necessary to achieve this.

The importance of a thorough examination of mast, spars, rigging and fittings cannot be overemphasised. Much of this equipment will be out of sight in the course of sailing, and while a wise skipper will send a crew member aloft before the onset of a severe blow, there are few real opportunities to check the mast and rigging as part of daily routine. Yet failure of any of this gear can be disastrous during a blow and can severely endanger the boat and her crew. A thorough check before purchase can at least indicate any major weaknesses aloft which can be rectified before the boat puts to sea. Or the sale can be abandoned and the search for a safer boat continued.

A relatively clear deck with sound hatches, halyards led back to the cockpit and small windows indicate a boat that is well designed to ride out a blow.

Going aloft in a bosun's chair is an alternative way of checking the above-deck fittings, but it is not as satisfactory as unstepping the mast and having everything down on the wharf where an experienced rigger can be called in if there are any doubts about the gear. The strength of spreaders, for example, is an important factor, for a collapsed spreader in a blow will almost certainly mean the loss of the mast. Yachts which are built for racing often save weight aloft by using lightweight fittings, notably spreaders, and for an ocean crossing it would be necessary to change or strengthen these.

The same applies to the rigging. Advice from an expert rigger will indicate the efficiency of the shrouds and stays, and also their possible life span. Plough steel wire gives plenty of indication that it is nearing its terminal point, but stainless steel rigging can snap without any signs of whiskering or wear. One broken stay when the boat is under pressure can mean the loss of everything above the deck line. A rigger will also indicate the age of the stainless steel wire, for this material is subject to fatigue, and age is an important factor in its potential life span.

54

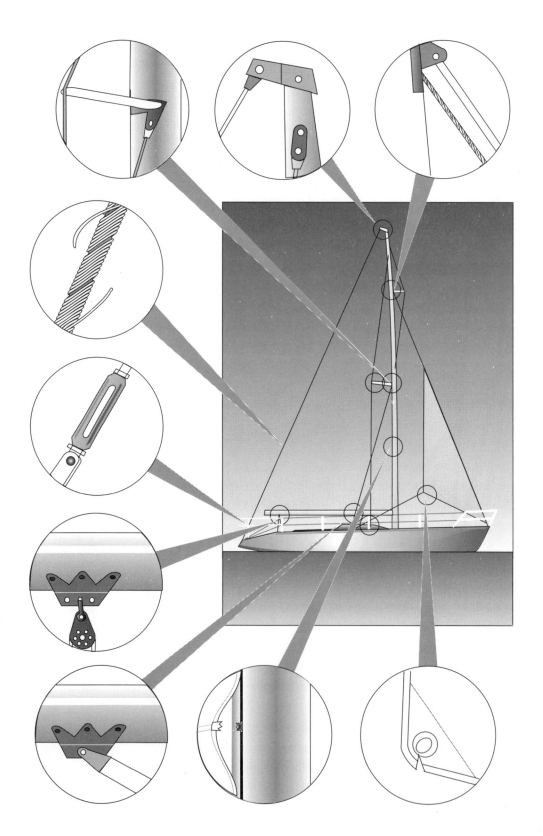

Sheaves for internal halyards are bunched at the top of the mast and these, too, need careful inspection. Wire halyards have a nasty habit of jumping off the sheave when it starts to wear, and jamming between the sheave and the throat of the fitting. A mainsail jammed at the top of the mast and unable to be lowered or reefed is not the most desirable of events with a storm moving in. Sending a crew member aloft under these conditions will not be appreciated by the crew, either. Indeed, this can create so dangerous a situation at sea, that many experienced ocean sailors will not tolerate internal halyards but use pre-stretched rope halyards outside the mast. These can easily be cut if the worst comes to the worst.

Corrosion around fittings on an aluminium mast can weaken the mast wall considerably, just as rot can weaken a timber mast. With most terminals, sheaves and winches made from metal these days, the possibility of corrosion from different metals coming into contact is very real, and can severely eat away the wall of an aluminium mast without showing a great deal of external damage. Only a thorough examination will indicate how bad this problem is. It can be avoided by mounting fittings on insulating material, but if corrosion has already taken hold, the damage may already be beyond repair. This problem rarely arises on timber masts since the timber itself acts as an insulator between metal fittings.

Although not always practical, unstepping the mast is the best way to check the condition of above-deck gear.

The importance of a thorough examination of mast, spars, rigging and fittings cannot be overemphasised.

57

Motors

When the chips are down (and perhaps the mast is down, too), often the only thing between disaster and survival is the motor. In powered vessels, of course, it is the key factor at all times, and no emphasis is needed on how important pre-purchase inspection is in this case. But much the same applies to the smaller auxiliary motors fitted to ocean-going yachts. When the going really gets tough, often the motor is the only means of avoiding disaster. A crew member overboard, the mast down, water in the hull; all these, and many more dramas, can make the use of the motor the difference between life and death. So when buying the boat, the motor must come in for close scrutiny.

The amount of power is important. This generally does not apply to motor yachts which have plenty of reserve power, but it does apply to yachts, where often the power unit is meant simply to give the boat enough manoeuvrability to get in and out of her mooring berth. Such power will not be sufficient to stem a strong wind or big sea, or swing the boat around to go back and pick up a crew member in the water. Nor will it get her off a lee shore when the mast and sails are gone. It must have sufficient power for all these eventualities and more. Purists may scorn the use of power on a sailing craft, but such scorn can turn to abject fear when there are no sails and disaster looms close.

As far as motor yacht owners are concerned, it is important to ensure that the boat has two motors. In a storm offshore, it is as easy for a motor yacht to lose one engine as it is for a sailing yacht to lose its mast. Without a second motor the boat is at the mercy of wind and sea; not a pleasant situation to be in as motor yachts do not ride as deep-hulled yachts when they are adrift without power.

Small auxiliary motors used aboard ocean-going yachts need to be sufficiently powerful to provide good backup when mast and sails go overboard. There may be quite a way to motor to reach safety.

Inside the hull

Although the outside of the boat is the part that carries the brunt of wind, sea and weather, the inside of the hull is always a good place to look for indications of possible stresses and strains affecting the hull structure. Water in the bilges, for example, must have entered the hull somewhere. Chances are it will have

seeped in the stern gland around the propeller shaft, and providing it is not too much, this is perfectly normal. On the other hand, if the stern gland is fairly tight, salt-water in the bilges could indicate some serious problems and you would start going over the hull with a fine-toothed comb to find out where it's getting in.

If it is fresh water (you have to taste it!) then there is a leak in the deck, hatches or windows, letting in rainwater, and this at least will make for discomfort for the crew, at worst could set up dry rot in timber fittings, even the hull if it is made from timber. These are the sort of indications which make an inspection of the inside of the hull a necessary part of determining whether the boat is seaworthy or not.

Big power boats need reliable motors; preferably diesel. Without sails, the safety of the boat and all on board will depend on the performance of the motors.

Timber hulls

As just mentioned, dry rot can be set up on the inside of a timber hull by fresh water leaks, and this is an insidious and dangerous pest. Even in fibreglass and metal hulls it is a nuisance as it slowly destroys wooden fittings, furnishings and the like. It also creates a musty and unpleasant smell inside the cabin areas. As a general

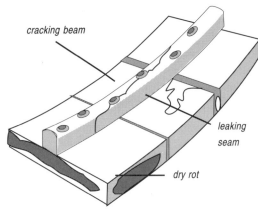

cracking beam

leaking seam

dry rot

Cracking of major structural members can indicate that the boat has been placed under heavy stress at some time, and these could lead to weakness later.

rule it appears as a white, powdery substance on the surface of the timber, but in its more insidious form it may show no outward signs, but quietly eat away the body of the timber, leaving nothing more than a thin veneer on the surface.

This is bad enough in terms of interior fittings and furnishings, but needless to say, it creates havoc if it gets into the hull. Like the toredo worm, it destroys the inner body of the timber, leaving the outer surface seemingly sound. Then one day the whole structure collapses inwards, sometimes with disastrous effects. Dry rot can be detected by tapping the surfaces, as described for the outside of the hull. When the rot is present the tapping produces a dull thud, as opposed to the normal ringing sound of the adjacent timbers.

Dry rot can only be caused by fresh water, the salt in sea water renders the fungus (for that is what it is) inoperable. Indeed, in the days of wooden decks, many seamen used constant washing down with salt water to prevent access of dry rot. However, salt water can cause wet rot, and a close inspection of the inside surfaces of a timber hull should be made, particularly in the bilge area, if there are signs of dampness anywhere.

Other problems with timber, such as cracking or leaking, are mostly superficial unless, of course, they occur in the underwater areas. Cracking of major structural members can indicate that the boat has been placed under heavy stress at some time, and these could lead to weakness later, but generally speaking, dry and wet rot are the two major danger factors to be looked for when examining the inside of a timber hull.

Fibreglass hulls

There are far fewer structural members in hulls of fibreglass structure, so extremes of stress are likely to be more obvious. Cracking of the hull structure or for that matter any part of the moulded lay-up should be treated with suspicion. On the other hand, crazing, which is usually in the form of patches of fine cracks, may not be so significant. Much depends on where the crazing occurs. 'Hot spots', such as beneath the mast step or where fittings are placed under strain, can sometimes indicate excessive stress in the form of crazing.

These must be treated with caution. Minor spots of crazed gelcoat may only indicate that the area has been given a hard bump with something, and this should not create a structural problem.

Salt water in the bilges can be simply from the stern gland, as described earlier, or it can indicate a damaged area in the hull. Skin fittings should be carefully examined as these are always subject to hot spots of stress where they pierce the fibreglass hull. Fresh water probably indicates leaking window or hatch seals, but should prompt a close examination of the whole deckhead area as well.

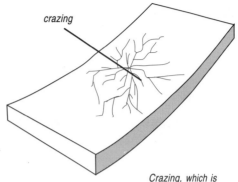

crazing

Crazing, which is usually in the form of patches of fine cracks, may or may not be significant. Much depends on where the crazing occurs.

Metal hulls

Here again, the water in the bilges can be traced either to an insignificant matter like a slack stern gland (easily fixed by repacking) or can indicate more serious problems. A careful check of the interior of the hull skin should be made for possible corrosion from galvanic action or cracked welding indicating hot spots of stress. Dents and other superficial damage rarely cause structural damage to a well-built metal boat although they can damage paint surfaces, allowing rust to get a hold.

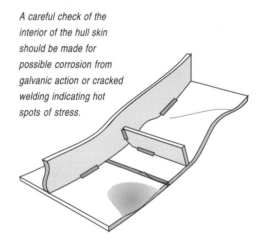

A careful check of the interior of the hull skin should be made for possible corrosion from galvanic action or cracked welding indicating hot spots of stress.

Concrete hulls

The main source of trouble with a concrete hull, other than the problems which affect hulls of any type, is damage to the plaster skin, allowing ingress of salt water into the metal mesh structure of the hull. While damage of this kind is most likely to occur on the outside of the hull, it is not unknown for a yacht that has been stranded on shoal ground to appear unscathed on the outside, but suffer interior cracking of the hull due to hogging or sagging stresses while on the ground.

The description given earlier in this chapter under 'Concrete Cancer' should leave no doubt in any prospective buyer's mind that a thorough inspection of the plaster skin, both inside and outside, is essential if this scourge is to be

61

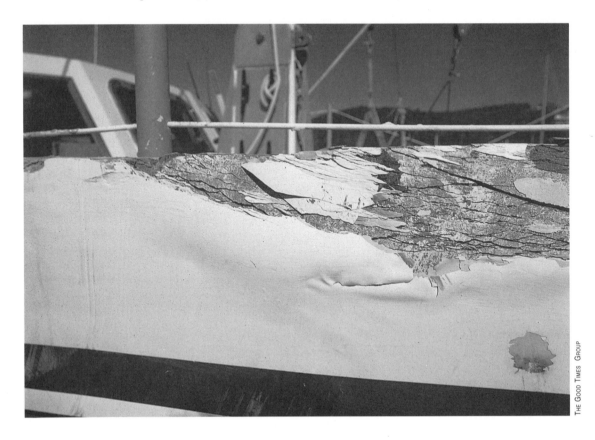

THE GOOD TIMES GROUP

On a ferro-cement yacht a point of impact may leave little indication of the damage on the outside, but suffer interior cracking and flacking of the cement with distortion of the reinforcing steel.

avoided. Otherwise, dry rot in timber fittings, rust or corrosion in metal fittings and the other factors that are encountered in all boats no matter what their construction, are the main factors to look for when checking on the structural detail on the inside of a concrete hull.

Summing up

The importance of a thorough examination before signing contracts for the purchase of any vessel cannot be overemphasised. Wherever possible, an expert in hull structure, such as a marine surveyor, marine engineer or naval architect should be engaged to undertake this examination. However, the points described above provide a fairly broad indication of the main structural problems that can be found and

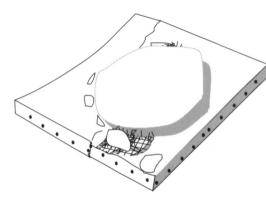

how to look for them. With or without the expert, most prospective purchasers like to run their eye over their potential acquisition, and knowing what to look for and where to look, can help quite a bit.

The boat must be taken out of the water for this inspection, as there is no way of telling what is going on below the waterline while she is afloat. A 'test run' is also a good idea, particularly in terms of testing the motors on a power vessel, and determining the sailing performance of a yacht. There are many individual and personal factors that must also be considered, of course, but these have no place in a book of this nature as they are effectively mostly cosmetic.

CHAPTER 4

The sea

Two main factors affect a boat during a blow: wind and water. Since these are both connected, and work together to create the sea conditions that are the major factor in a vessel riding out a storm, it is worth studying them briefly as a means of better understanding what they are all about. The wind we will deal with later; of prime importance is the sea-that restless medium that covers some 75 per cent of the world's surface and which has held a fascination for humans since the dawn of time.

Wave formation

Waves are created by the transfer of energy from wind to water, and the amount of energy involved can be quite surprising. For example, a wind blowing at 20 knots across a smooth surface creates friction or drag that will generate a force of some 10 tonnes per square kilometre. This force will increase as the surface of the water ruffles, forming an uneven surface which in turn creates more friction.

This surface friction between the wind and the water creates the first ripples and as the wind increases, the waves gather more energy from the wind and start to build in size. A little of the friction will be reduced as the waves begin to move, but this is insufficient to counteract the enormous transfer of energy and the waves will continue to build as the wind continues to blow. When the waves have reached a size where they are capable of absorbing the wind's energy they will not grow any further.

This is the basic theory; in practice there are other factors which affect the formation, shape and size of waves, but that is getting into technical detail too complex for a book such as this.

Wave shape

In the open sea, the movement of water in a wave form is orbital close to the surface. This can be easily visualised by watching the movement of a cork floating in a wave pattern. As a wave advances under the cork it will move backwards and

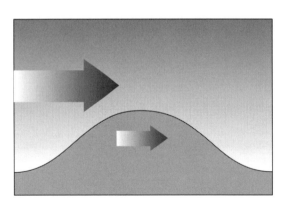

The surface friction between the wind and the water creates the waves. A little of the friction is reduced as the waves move, but this is insufficient to counteract the enormous transfer of energy

In the open sea, the movement of water in a wave form is orbital close to the surface.

The movement in the wave is confined mainly to the surface or the water immediately below the surface; the size of the circular orbit decreases rapidly with depth.

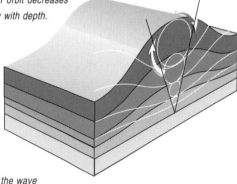

When the wave moves into water around half a wavelength in depth, the lower portion of the orbital movement is impeded by the frictional resistance of the sea bed and causes the shape of the wave to change.

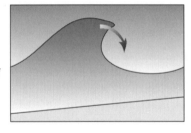

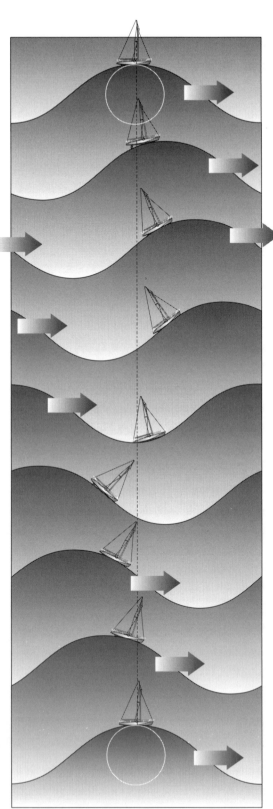

down into the trough ahead of the next wave. At the bottom of the trough it will reach the lowest point of the circle. As the face of the next wave moves towards it, the cork will rise and start to move forward with the wave. As it tops the crest, the cork will be at the top of the circle and moving at maximum speed ahead. Then, as the wave passes under it the circle is completed and the cork moves backwards and downwards to begin the next cycle.

When the full circle has been completed, the cork will be almost exactly in the spot where in began the circle in the previous trough. There is a slight forward movement due to the wave's motion and wind effect, but in deep water it is negligible; an interesting fact when considered in the context of a crew member overboard and the manoeuvring of the boat necessary to pick him or her up.

This movement in the wave is confined mainly to the surface or the water immediately below the surface; the size of the circular orbit decreases rapidly with depth and disappears altogether at little more than half a wavelength below the surface. This explains why waves in shallow water have a different shape to those in deeper water and in particular explains why waves break on a beach or shoal patch.

As the wave moves into water around half a wavelength in depth, the lower portion of the orbital movement is impeded by the frictional resistance of the sea bed and causes the shape of the wave to change. If the beach continues to shallow, the circle is disrupted right to the surface and the wave literally trips over its own feet, breaking as surf in the shallows.

Fetch

Another factor affecting the shape of a wave is the distance over the water that the wind blows, known as the 'fetch'. In the lee of a high cliff there will be only small waves, if any. As the wind blows to seaward across a long fetch, the size of the waves will pick up because of the transfer of wind energy described earlier.

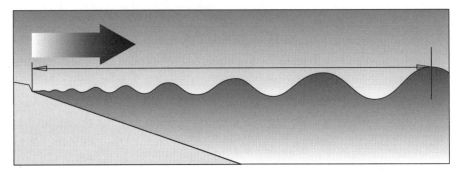

As the wind blows, the size of the waves will pick up.

The maximum wave height will be reached well offshore at a point determined by the strength of the wind and the depth of the water.

Because the wind does not blow at a consistent strength (especially when blowing off the land), the waves will not be of even shape or size. Some will be large and some smaller and they may take a number of different forms. However, as the wind continues to blow, the smaller waves absorb less energy than the large waves and so tend to become lost or absorbed in the general sea pattern formed by the larger waves.

If the wind shifts, as it often does, then the sea pattern becomes more confused as waves created by the new wind direction, cross the path of those already in motion. The passing of a frontal system with its dramatic wind change can create chaotic sea conditions. Likewise, the eye of a cyclone, where extremely high winds can switch direction across the compass in a matter of a few hours, may well resemble the inside of a giant cauldron as the seas frantically try to find some consistent direction from the winds that drive them.

Wave effect on small craft

Most seaworthy yachts can handle sea conditions encountered in normal sailing, even when riding out a gale. A well-designed, well-found vessel can cope with most waves other than perhaps the extremes encountered in a cyclone or hurricane, when the boat is overwhelmed by the sheer size of the seas. But then, no skipper worth his salt would take his boat into waters where these storms are in season. In normal ocean-crossing passages, deep-water waves of any size should not create problems for a seaworthy hull.

It is the shape of the wave rather than the size that can create discomfort and sometimes danger. Even in the 'Roaring Forties' of the Southern Ocean, where the largest seas in the world are recorded, small craft can sail quite safely under most conditions. These huge seas roll around the world with no interference from landmasses, but because of the depth of water they develop a long wavelength, so creating undulating 'hills' of water with a moderate gradient. Although frightening in size, these waves present relatively little risk of serious danger. The yacht literally climbs up one slope and slides down the other; a stomach-churning roller coaster ride, maybe, but often safer than riding the steep seas that can occur within sight of a home port.

This is where seas do become dangerous: when they run out of the deep water of the oceans and into the relatively shallow areas of the continental shelf. A classic example concerns the giant Southern Ocean waves described earlier. In

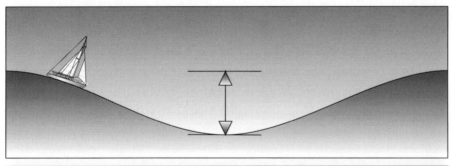

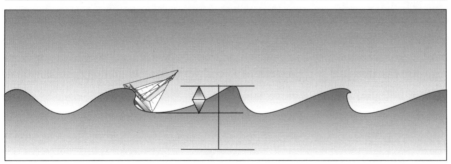

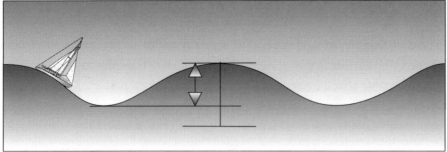

It is the shape of the wave rather than its size that creates problems for seagoing crafts. Small boats are actually safer and more confortable in the big, but well-spaced rollers of deep ocean than in the shorter, steeper seas created by shallow water close to the coast.

the Roaring forties, the big, but 'gentle giant' waves roll around the world creating no real problems because of the deep water beneath them. Then they approach the continental shelf, which runs out from the southern tip of South America, and the shallow water drags them up into fiendish monsters. This is the notorious Cape Horn. Sea conditions in these areas can be highly dangerous even to giant ships, leave alone small yachts.

Apart from the effect of shallow water, the wind blowing over a long fetch also increases the size of the waves, as described earlier, until a maximum height is reached, depending on the length of the fetch and the strength of the wind. In the open ocean, there is mostly a very long fetch, so when the wind blows for some time, the waves build both in size and gradient.

As the wind continues, so the seas build, and this is the scenario that creates gale conditions with big, steep seas, where yachts and other small craft are forced to take action to ride it out, either by heaving to, or by adopting one of the other tactics described in Chapter 9. It is important to note that these sea conditions, however bad, will not be avoided by running in to the coast. Indeed, the reverse is the case, for the shallow nature of inshore waters aggravate the offshore sea conditions, creating even steeper and more dangerous waves. This is one of a number of reasons why a boat caught out at sea should never attempt to run into the coast for shelter.

Tide and current effect

There are many other factors which affect the shape of a wave, and most of these are described earlier in this chapter. In inshore waters tides and currents can have a considerable effect, indeed, they can create waves of their own. Crossing a bar in certain conditions of wind and tide, for example, can be a particularly unpleasant form of maritime suicide, as can entering a harbour or river.

When a fast movement of water, such as a tide or current, encounters a moving wave head on, it causes the wave to rear up and develop a steep gradient. When the tide and waves are running in the same direction, the wavelength is extended and the gradient of the wave reduced. But when the seas are running against the tide, the old proverb of immovable objects and irresistible forces comes into play and violent sea conditions develop.

A fast flowing contra-current causes waves to build up and form steep faces. This is the danger associated with the entrance to big rivers.

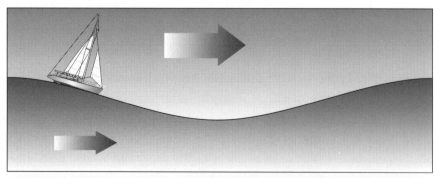

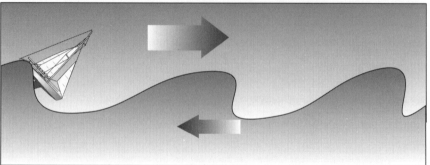

This phenomenon creates the need for great care when negotiating river mouths or other coastal areas where fast run-out of tide or currents may be encountered. It is also another reason why it is safer to stay out at sea when a blow moves in. The strong wind whipping up big onshore seas, the shallow waters of a river mouth exaggerating their steepness, and a strong run-out of tide through a river or harbour mouth is a sure recipe for danger. The seas pile up into a maelstrom of steep, breaking waves which usually form across the entrance, making it extremely dangerous, if not impossible, to make into harbour. This notorious bar condition is encountered at the mouth of many harbours and river estuaries.

Conversely, if the tide is flooding, the movement of water into the river mouth tempers the steepness and anger of the onshore waves and makes an entry more possible. Seafarers with local knowledge can then make into port, even in a blow, providing they time their run correctly. But the emphasis is on local knowledge, for the timing of the run-in is critical and in some places the tide allows only an hour or even less in which conditions are suitable for an entry .

Similar conditions can develop where there is a fast run of current around a point of land or between islands. The uncomfortable waters off the tip of South Africa are partly the result of the Aghullas Current streaming southwards around the Cape and striking the big rollers of the Roaring Forties moving in from the west.

Bombora

Called a bombora in the Pacific, this wave phenomenon is well known across the world by a number of different names. It is encountered mostly close to coastlines, although it may also be found in the open sea where shoal patches or reefs are located. It is an extension of the phenomenon which occurs when large waves move into shallow water, described earlier. This time the waves are moving across a shoal area where normally there may sufficient water to prevent the waves building, but when the big seas develop as the result of high winds, they rear up in the shallow water over the shoal or reef, and create hazardous conditions even for sizeable boats.

The insidious aspect of a bombora is that it can be hard to spot. To begin with it may be in an isolated spot, well away from any other shoal regions, perhaps even in deep water where underwater peaks can sometimes create bomboras. Also, when approached from windward only the back of the wave can be seen; the rearing face may be hidden. A yacht running before the wind may not see the

The broken waters of an offshore bombora indicate danger of some kind and must be given a wide berth.

turbulence until too late to avoid the danger, and when running before a blow, disaster can strike very quickly. Because of the steepness of the breaking wave and the shallow water over the shoal, the odds of getting out of a bombora in one piece are not good.

As a general rule the reef or shoal patch is marked on the chart, often with the symbol for 'overfalls' on it. While overfalls are more often the result of tidal or current phenomena, the effect of a bombora can be similar to that of severe overfalls and the result can be just as devastating. These hazards should be given a clear berth, especially when riding out a storm or in big seas.

Shore turbulence

This is a phenomenon which occurs a great deal along coastlines where steep cliffs drop sheer into the sea or where big breakwaters or some other obstruction sticks out to seaward. It is particularly severe on a coastline which faces directly towards an open ocean and has deep water right up to the foot of the cliffs. In normal wind and weather conditions there is no problem for well-found yachts. Indeed, with offshore winds, the conditions close under the lee of the cliffs are often like the proverbial millpond.

But with strong onshore winds driving big ocean rollers against the cliffs, extremely dangerous seas develop which can overwhelm even the most seaworthy of craft. Unimpeded by shallow water, the big seas roll right into the shore and hurl themselves against the cliff or obstruction, then 'ricochet' back into the oncoming waves behind. The huge power of both the oncoming and the rebounding waves creates a maelstrom of turbulent water that can reach tens of metres into the air and make short work of even sizeable vessels, sending them hurtling out of control against the cliffs or breakwater.

Here again is a very valid reason to stay out at sea when a blow develops. While confined only to certain areas of the coast, boats making inshore to shelter from a blow can find themselves totally overwhelmed by seas far more savage than those farther out to sea. The natural urge to make into port to ride out a storm has resulted in disaster for many small craft (and not a few big ships). It may be less comfortable to ride it out in the open ocean, but it is mostly much safer and a well-found boat will survive with ease, whereas closing with the coast can spell doom for even the biggest and strongest.

CHAPTER 5

Wind and weather

'There is only one way to beat the weather-stay one step ahead of it.' These wise words are from an old salt and bear thinking about, particularly where small craft and offshore waters are concerned. It is the *raison d'etre* of weather forecasting; knowing what is coming provides an opportunity to prepare for it before it arrives. Such information is useful for farmers and others who make their living from the land. But it is more than useful to sailors, to whom it can mean the difference between life and death.

Technology has done much to make life easier for those who daily challenge the elements, and weather satellites, radio forecasts, weather faxes and the like provide the means of keeping that all-important one step ahead of the weather. Advance warnings of approaching storms or other disturbances allow time to prepare or perhaps avoid conditions which may threaten the boat and her crew. Where sailors once depended on sky signs which gave them only limited time to batten down, now regular forecasts can warn sometimes days ahead of approaching problems.

The synoptic chart

The basis of all surface weather patterns, the synoptic chart is an analysis of weather records taken at regular intervals at specified points across the world. By plotting these records on a chart, the development and movement of major systems affecting the weather can be followed by experts at the meteorological bureaus and the progress of potentially dangerous systems studied so that warning can be issued in good time. Most countries have their own synoptic charting departments. Most cover fairly wide areas, as the weather patterns are quite extensive and can cover an large continent.

The synoptic chart consists of a map of the area covered, say a specific country and the areas that immediately surround it, onto which is superimposed the recorded information gathered from numerous reporting stations scattered

A typical synoptic chart, showing the distribution of pressure gradients and fronts. Such charts are invaluable to offshore sailors.

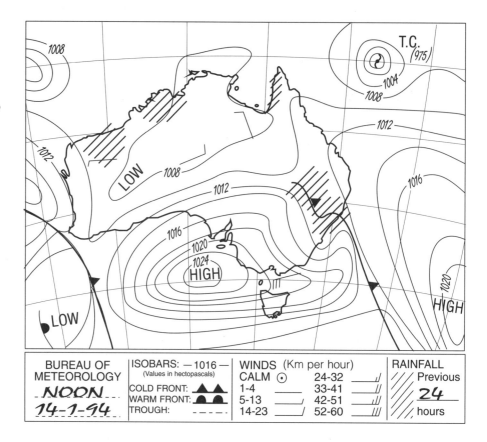

| BUREAU OF METEOROLOGY *NOON* *14-1-94* | ISOBARS: —1016— (Values in hectopascals) COLD FRONT: WARM FRONT: TROUGH: - - - - | WINDS (Km per hour) CALM ⊙   24-32 1-4 ___   33-41 5-13 ___/   42-51 14-23 ___/   52-60 ___/// | RAINFALL /// Previous *24* // hours |

across the area. This information may include barometric pressure gradients, usually represented by contour lines called isobars, frontal information in the form of symbols on the chart, and in some cases, wind and cloud details. Since the pressure systems are the main controlling factors of surface weather, and all weather patterns move in a roughly west-to-east direction, this information can be analysed from the synoptic chart to indicate the nature of approaching weather

Weatherfax

Synoptic charts can be received by boats at sea through a weatherfax, an instrument which is now a fairly standard fitting for offshore yachts making extensive passages. This is an adaptation of the normal fax system used in offices. Facsimile transmissions of synoptic charts and other related information are made at regular intervals from broadcast stations on shore. TV weather forecasts and daily newspapers also carry synoptic charts.

The movement of pressure systems and any phenomenon within the weather

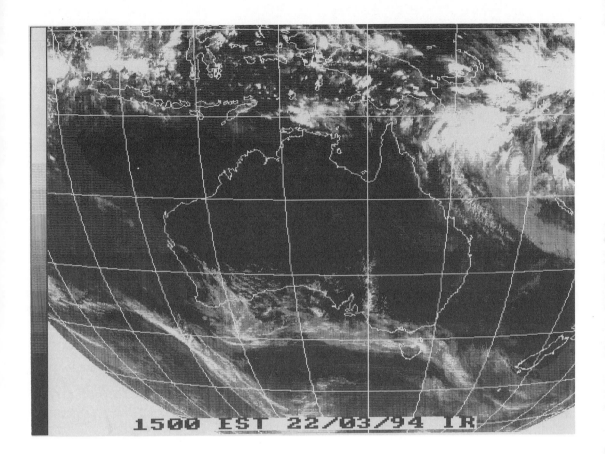

1500 EST 22/03/94 IR

pattern can be determined from a consecutive series of synoptic charts if they are available, while the approaching weather can be fairly accurately determined from individual charts. Using the weatherfax ensures that a continuous supply of such charts is provided and this enables the approaching weather patterns to be plotted with a great degree of accuracy.

Fascimile weather charts or satellite pictures can be obtained at sea providing the boat is within reach of a transmitting station. These can asist greatly in accurately forecasting approaching

Basically, the synoptic chart indicates the position, intensity and extent of high and low-pressure systems, the two main factors influencing surface weather. Surrounding the pressure systems are the contours of the isobars, which give an indication of the wind direction and strength across the systems. Frontal systems, occlusions and any phenomena which may affect the weather patterns may also be included. Local disturbances are not usually shown.

Due to the rotation of the earth, the pressure systems travel in a roughly easterly direction across the chart, so a picture of approaching weather can be gained by studying the area to the westwards of the boat's position and watching for changes as it moves closer. The importance of a progressive series of synoptic charts is obvious, for depressions can fill, troughs and ridges can form and other characteristics of the systems can develop in a matter of only a few hours. By studying a progression of synoptic charts spaced perhaps four to six hours apart, such changes can often be spotted as they occur. While local phenomena and factors such as a nearby coast can affect the weather, as a general rule a fair idea of the oncoming pattern can be made from the synoptic charts. Certainly, any major weather patterns, such as gales or severe fronts, will show up in good time for you to take the necessary precautions.

Other information carried by the synoptic chart may include wind direction, speed arrows, barometric pressure and an indication of weather conditions, as well as any information relative to the movement of cyclones, hurricanes, typhoons and other dangerous systems. Not all transmissions carry full information; much depends on the region of the world and its vulnerability to dangerous weather conditions.

Isobars and winds

The contour lines of the isobars have a variety of purposes of which two are important in determining approaching weather. First, they indicate the location of each pressure system, which in turn gives a fairly accurate indication of the sort of weather in the area. Second, they indicate the approximate direction and strength of the winds at any given point.

The pressure systems and their effect on the weather are described later, but of prime importance to any sailor is the strength and direction of the wind and particularly the possible onset of any gales or other form of strong winds and dirty weather. This is where the isobars are handy. Since winds rotate in a roughly clockwise direction around a low-pressure system and anti-clockwise direction around a high-pressure system (in the southern hemisphere, the opposite applies to the northern hemisphere), an indication of the direction of the wind can be gained by the direction of the isobars at the boat's position.

In actual fact there is a tendency for the winds to angle slight inwards towards the centre across low-pressure isobars and outwards from the centre in high-pressure isobars and this should be taken into account when assessing any approaching wind changes from the isobars on the synoptic chart.

Similarly, the spacing between the isobars indicates the pressure gradient between high and low-pressure systems in much the same way that contour lines on a topographical map indicate the gradient of a hillside or mountain. The closer together the isobars the steeper the gradient and the stronger the winds, and vice versa.

High-pressure systems, being the 'fair weather' systems, usually have well-

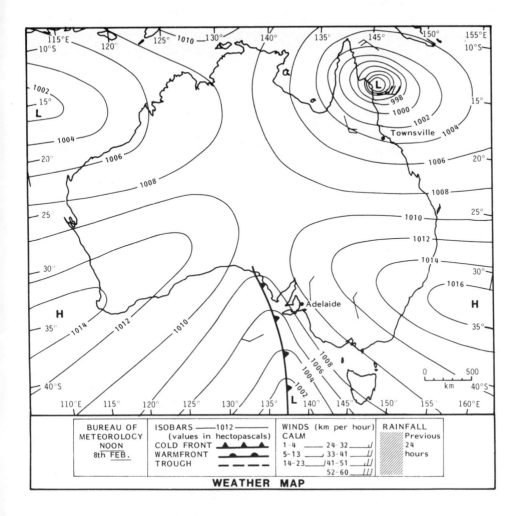

| BUREAU OF METEOROLOGY NOON 8th FEB. | ISOBARS ——1012—— (values in hectopascals) COLD FRONT ▲▲▲ WARMFRONT ●●● TROUGH – – – | WINDS (km per hour) CALM 1·4 ——— 24-32 ——⌐ 5-13 ——⌐ 33-41 ——⌐⌐ 14-23 ——⌐⌐ 41-51 ——⌐⌐ 52-60 ——⌐⌐⌐ | RAINFALL ▨ Previous 24 hours |

WEATHER MAP

spaced isobars, indicating light to moderate winds as the high-pressure system moves across the ocean. Low-pressure systems are more likely to have their isobars ringed closely around the centre, indicating stronger winds which, as the depression deepens, can start to resemble a whirlpool. When a tight series of concentric rings appear on the synoptic chart it is time for alarm bells to start ringing, as these indicate very intense depressions, usually associated with cyclones, hurricanes or typhoons.

It is not hard to appreciate the value of a synoptic chart to offshore sailors, since approaching winds-and particularly 'nasty' systems such as cyclones-can be predicted fairly well in advance as they move in from a westerly direction. While local phenomena, such as land and sea breezes, can upset even the most carefully prepared forecast, as a general rule it is possible to predict with reasonable accuracy the change in approaching weather conditions from the configurations of the synoptic chart.

The intensity of a cyclone is easily seen by the closeness of the isobars on a synoptic chart.

79

High-pressure systems

As mentioned, these are generally termed 'fair weather' systems because high pressure generally brings stable, fine weather patterns. They spread over a wide area and brings light to moderate winds, fair to fine weather and fairly pleasant weather conditions. Winds rotate in a roughly clockwise direction around the isobars in the northern hemisphere and anti-clockwise in the southern hemisphere, radiating slightly outwards from the centre. Severe wind conditions are rarely encountered within the high-pressure system, unless they are created by some local phenomenon. In warm climates it is often the harbinger of sea breezes near a coastline.

High-pressure systems, usually have well-spaced isobars, indicating light to moderate winds as the high-pressure system moves across the ocean. Low-pressure systems are more likely to have their isobars ringed closely around the centre, indicating stronger winds which, as the depression deepens, can start to resemble a whirlpool.

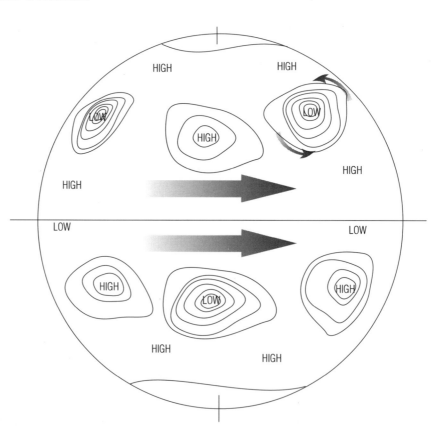

Low-pressure systems

These are the 'dirty' systems, usually associated with unstable, unpleasant weather, with isobars closer together, indicating stronger winds and inclement weather. Winds rotate roughly along the isobars in an anti-clockwise direction in the northern hemisphere, clockwise in the southern hemisphere, bearing slightly inwards towards the centre. In this system any number of 'nasties' can be encountered, particularly cold and warm fronts, occlusions and phenomenon such as line squalls and willy-willies.

Unpleasant weather, building often to gale force, is the norm for low-pressure or depression systems which, when carried to their extreme in tropical climates in their season, can become tropical revolving storms (cyclones, hurricanes, typhoons), the ultimate bad weather horror for sailors.

Making a weather forecast

Away from the coast and any local anomalies which may upset the standard weather pattern, it is fairly easy and reasonably accurate to make a forecast of the weather likely to be experienced by the boat over the following twenty-four hours or more. A series of synoptic charts, as mentioned, will indicate any development of weather patterns, and with each a plot of the boat's position and the likely weather she will experience can be made. In this way a close eye on approaching weather can be maintained with reasonable accuracy.

Method
Take the last synoptic chart received by weatherfax and plot on it the boat's position. For the purpose of exercise, let's assume the chart is the one illustrated in Figure 1 and the position of the boat is plotted at point A.

A track is then laid in a roughly westward direction across the chart from point A. This represents the likely path of the boat through the system as it moves eastwards. From this a projected weather forecast, assuming the boat to be in the southern hemisphere, could be as follows.

As the system moves eastwards, the boat's relative position will move westwards through the outer isobars of the system along the track from point A. Depending on the speed at which the system is moving, which can be ascertained from a previous series of weatherfaxes, the wind could be expected initially to blow from the north-east at a moderate strength.

As the depression moves over the boat, the wind will veer to the east and increase as the isobars get closer together. When the boat is close to the centre of the depression the wind will be easterly, quite strong, then will start to move into the south-east, veering more to the south and easing as the isobars open up. When the boat moves out of the low-pressure system altogether at point B, the wind should be south to south-westerly and moderating.

81

As the system moves eastwards, the boat's relative position will move westwards through the outer isobars of the system along the track from point A.

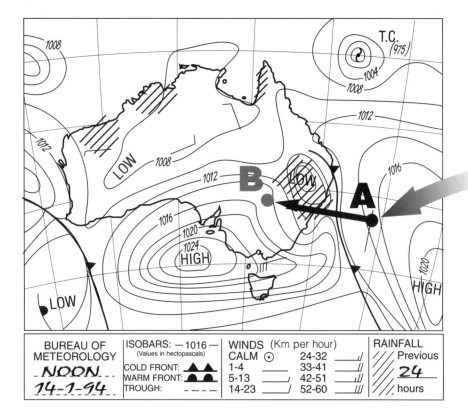

| BUREAU OF METEOROLOGY *NOON* *14-1-94* | ISOBARS: — 1016 — (Values in hectopascals) COLD FRONT: ▲▲ WARM FRONT: ●● TROUGH: - - - - | WINDS (Km per hour) CALM ⊙ 1-4 5-13 14-23 | 24-32 33-41 42-51 52-60 | RAINFALL ///Previous *24* /// hours |

Since a low-pressure cell is usually followed by a high-pressure system, the ensuing weather can be expected to improve with fine conditions and lighter winds developing as the boat moves into the high-pressure region. By repeating the plot with future weatherfax charts, a progressive forecast can be developed through all approaching weather systems.

Local weather phenomena

The synoptic chart reveals only the pattern of pressure systems located close to the surface of the globe, and while this is the area of most concern to sailors, the weather can be affected quite considerably by outside factors such as high-altitude conditions and local phenomena. The so-called 'jet stream' that affects aircraft with often extremely strong wind patterns is a typical example of high-altitude conditions which do not appear on the synoptic chart. Fortunately for seagoing craft, the jet stream does not usually affect surface weather either, but some high-altitude weather can have quite a considerable influence on surface conditions. However, there is no way of predicting this as synoptic charts do not carry information about high-altitude conditions.

Local phenomena are also excluded from the synoptic chart, but these are often easy to predict as they follow established patterns and are often restricted to specific areas. Cold and warm fronts are shown on the chart, but it is debatable whether these fall into the category of 'local' conditions as they can occur anywhere and travel for quite some distance. However, their effect is local so they will be mentioned in this section.

All over the world local phenomena affect the weather patterns in some way or another. Classic cases such as the Mistral in Mediterranean waters and the Southerly Buster off the east coast of Australia are well documented and very predictable. In other cases, weather conditions may be affected to varying degrees by the presence of warm or cold water currents, high coastal mountain ranges and other geographical features. Only local knowledge will enable the local weather conditions which are the result of such phenomena to be predicted with any degree of accuracy.

Land and sea breezes

Unquestionably, the best known weather phenomena in warmer climates are the wind patterns known as land and sea breezes. They occur in tropical and sub-tropical climates and in some temperate regions where in summer the temperature rises to a fairly high level. It involves the development of thermal activity over the land and so is restricted to waters fairly close to shore-perhaps only a few nautical miles to seaward of the coast.

It begins around the middle of a warm to hot, sunny day as the land starts to heat up. Warm thermal air rises off the land, creating a vacuum beneath it which draws cool air in from the sea to fill the vacuum. The result: a light, steady breeze blowing onshore from the sea.

As the heat of the day increases, so the thermal cycle develops and the gentle breeze off the sea increases as the hot air rises faster over the land and the cool sea air rushes in to fill the vacuum. By mid-afternoon a moderate to strong onshore breeze has settled in and continues until the sun starts to lose its heat in the evening. This is the 'sea breeze' and is popular with sailors for its predictability, its strength and its consistency. Weekend yacht races in most coastal waters throughout the tropical and sub-tropical world enjoy the benefits of this steady breeze.

As the land cools down during the hours of darkness, the procedure is reversed. The sea retains its heat throughout the night so that by the early hours

The land heats up during the day, creating thermal updrafts which in turn draw air from the sea. As the day gets hotter, the air drawn from the sea becomes a significant breeze blowing onshore — the Sea Breeze.

During the night the cycle is reversed. The land cools down quicker than the sea, so the warm thermals rise off the sea, and draws a cool breeze from the land — the Land Breeze.

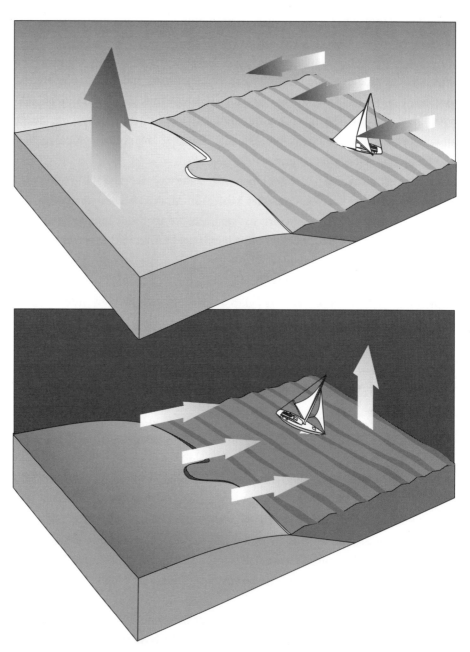

of the morning, warm thermals are rising off the sea, creating a vacuum that draws a steady breeze off the land to fill it. This is the 'land breeze' part of the phenomena, and while the offshore breeze at night is mostly much lighter than the onshore sea breeze of the day, it is nonetheless consistent and steady; a factor appreciated by inshore sailors working along a coastline in the dark hours. With the rising of the sun the whole cycle begins again.

84

This is a consistent, predictable and useful wind pattern that has been used probably since seafaring began. Indeed, windjammers of the 'tall ships' era used it frequently. Because of their inability to point high into the wind, they relied mostly on following winds to get them across the world's oceans. Then, when close to shore, they used the land and sea breezes to navigate into and out of port. During the day, the sea breeze provided a following wind to take them into harbour, and during the night the land breeze gave them a following wind to put out to sea again.

Fronts

Fronts are not strictly local phenomenon, they are part of normal weather patterns and exist in different climatic and geographic locations all round the world. They form within low-pressure systems, but rarely stay with the system for very long. They tend to become accepted as local conditions since they create brief and sudden changes of weather and can be limited to a quite localised region. Certainly, from a practical point of view, experiencing the passage of a cold front is not dissimilar sometimes to encountering a localised 'nasty'. Frontal systems

The "roll" of cloud often associated with a cold front gives good visual warning of the approaching turbulence.

such as the Australian 'Southerly Buster' have become accepted as a local weather phenomenon.

This is because the passage of a front — particularly a cold front — is usually of short duration and brings sudden, often dramatic changes of weather. The normal changes of weather due to the passage of pressure systems takes place over a period of many hours, even days. A gale, for example, whipped up by an intense depression, will build gradually, often giving a couple of day's notice of its approach. By contrast, a cold front can scream out of an almost clear blue sky only minutes after its telltale cloud formation passes overhead. A gale will settle in and blow for a few days, whereas the main impact of a cold front will be over in minutes and may be totally gone in an hour.

Warm fronts

These are the milder of the two main frontal systems and occur when warm air moves over a region of cool or cold air. The demarcation between the warm and cold air is in the form of a modest gradient with the frontal surface angled forward in the direction the front is travelling. This low or moderate gradient means that the arrival of the front is fairly slow with plenty of advance warning. It will be marked on the faxed synoptic chart as a curved line, usually radiating around the centre of a low-pressure system, with a series of black semicircles along its forward surface indicating the position of the frontal surface at ground level. The approach of the warm front is indicated by a slow build-up of mid-level and low cloud, usually accompanied by drizzle which can turn to steady rain as the front passes over. Winds are light and there is usually no dramatic change in conditions, although a slow rise in temperature will become apparent when the

The approach of the warm front is indicated by a slow build-up of mid-level and low cloud, usually accompanied by drizzle which can turn to steady rain as the front passes over

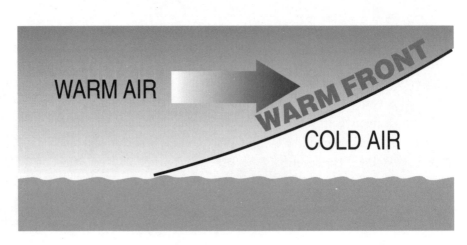

WARM AIR

WARM FRONT

COLD AIR

frontal surface moves past. Because of its docile nature, the warm front holds little fear for sailors; indeed, as often as not it is welcomed for its increase in surrounding air temperature.

Cold fronts

These can be quite severe systems and create dangerous situations for boats not expecting them or not prepared for the savagery they can initiate. The distinctive turbulence of a cold front is created by a wedge of cold air pushing under and forcing upwards a layer of warm air. As the two different air masses mix, extreme turbulence is developed and indicated by massive, 'boiling' cumulus rising into the sky not unlike the aftermath of an atomic bomb explosion. These conditions are exceptionally dangerous to aircraft, who fly around them, and can also create savage conditions at sea level. While there is often no time for boats to take avoiding action, it is important that the approach of a cold front is noted and preparations made to ride out the blow that will arrive with it.

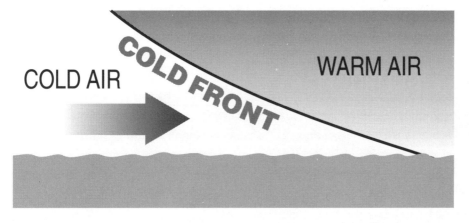

COLD AIR   COLD FRONT   WARM AIR

The distinctive turbulence of a cold front is created by a wedge of cold air pushing under and forcing upwards a layer of warm air. As the two different air masses mix, extreme turbulence is developed and indicated by massive, 'boiling' cumulus rising into the sky.

Sky signs indicate the approach of a cold front fairly well in advance. By day the first signs are bands of high cirrus moving in from the south or west and gradually covering the sky. Middle and lower level clouds soon follow, usually with the distinctive 'towering' cumulus rearing high into the background. Thunder and lightning will be evident as the front approaches and the sky will darken ominously. The severity of the front will depend to a great extent on the air temperature, so if the air is steamy and tropical, then the front can expected to be fairly dramatic. By night, the pyrotechnic display of the lightning is the best indicator that a front is moving in, and is quite unmistakeable.

From first signs, it can take between two and six hours for the front to strike, depending on conditions which control its speed across the surface. The air becomes heavy and hot and often the wind dies shortly before the front strikes- the proverbial lull before the storm! Often a cold front will adopt a 'line squall' format which can be seen approaching across the water as a maelstrom of white, churned water stretching across the surface of the sea. A roll of low black cloud in a line across the sky is another indicator that sometimes reveals the approach of the front.

In hot temperatures, the cold front usually strikes with a sudden and savage change in wind direction and strength as well as an immediate drop in temperature. Within minutes the wind speed can reach gale force and beyond, which indicates the importance of reducing sail and preparing the boat before it strikes. The wind will settle into its new direction and then proceed to 'blow the surface off the sea' as one old salt puts it. Blown spray and rain can reduce visibility to zero, which creates another dangerous aspect of this phenomenon, particularly if the boat is navigating close inshore, or in shipping lanes. Radar is virtually useless under these conditions.

Then as quickly as it came, the wind will ease. Just how long the blow will last depends on the conditions that exist when it arrived. An old sailor's jingle has a great deal of merit in this regard:

Quick to come, soon past.
Slow to start, long last.

The massive turbulence of very hot air being pushed up by the cold wedge moves forward quickly, so the more violent the storm, the sooner, as a general rule, it moderates and eases away. Like the proverbial storm in a teacup, a cold front can pass over with winds racing from 0 to 50 knots and back to 0 inside an hour or so. On the other hand, it can sometimes settle in to a moderate blow, after the initial squalls pass over, and continue for quite some time.

Obviously then, a cold front is not to be ignored. The appearance of the tell-tale curved line with black triangles along its leading edge, radiating out of the centre of a depression on a synoptic chart, should ring alarm bells in the mind of any skipper aboard any small craft at sea. A careful watch on the sky signs as the storm approaches will usually indicate its severity, and steps can be taken to prepare the boat for whatever arrives. Since cold fronts can be unpredictable, it is probably safest to be prepared for the worst; shaking out a reef in a sail is much easier than trying to throw one in after the storm has arrived.

The typical anvil shape of the violent Cumulonimbus or "thunderhead" cloud. These storm clouds are often associated with strong cold fronts.

CHAPTER 6

Cyclones, hurricanes and typhoons

Correctly known as 'tropical revolving storms', these are the most feared of all storm systems at sea. Yachts and small craft rarely survive a passage through one of these. Fortunately they are confined mostly to the tropical and sub-tropical belt around the world and rarely retain their savagery when they move out of that region.

Tropical revolving storms

In basic form, a tropical revolving storm (TRS) is simply a very deep depression, and is marked on the synoptic chart as such-a series of very close isobar circles resembling an intense whirlpool swirling anti-clockwise in the northern hemisphere and clockwise in the southern hemisphere. However, there the semblance ends, for the depth of the depression is such that in this system the mercury almost drops out the bottom of the barometer, and the winds are magnified beyond human belief. The resulting seas are massive and often tear around in confused disorder since the wind shifts constantly as the storm moves rapidly across the ocean surface. Such waves create a maelstrom in which even giant ocean-going ships have foundered; yachts and small craft have no chance.

The analogy of a whirlpool, mentioned in relation to the synoptic chart representation, holds good for the storm itself. The eye is relatively calm, while winds rotate around it at phenomenal speeds, creating a vortex somewhat akin to that of a huge whirlpool in the sky. The eye may extend over a relatively small area, but the storm itself may radiate over 400 kilometres or more and wind speeds may reach 250 kilometres per hour. It moves across the ocean surface at speeds up to 20 knots, which in itself is a good reason why small craft at sea must be aware of the formation of a TRS long before it reaches their vicinity. Outrunning such a storm is not often a practical possibility.

Path of the storm

If there is anything good to be said about a TRS it is that generally speaking it follows a predetermined track. Unfortunately this is not totally reliable and not a few meteorologists have been caught unawares by the storm doing what it is not expected to do. But as a general rule, the formation, track and disintegration of a TRS follow a fairly well-defined track.

As a general rule, the formation, track and disintegration of a TRS follow a fairly well-defined track

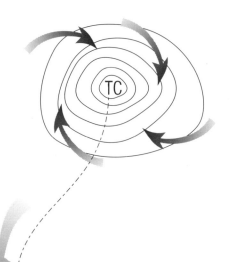

Most form in the latitude belt between 5 and 10 degrees north and south of the equator; few form inside the latitude of 5 degrees. Created as a result of a cyclonic disturbance, the TRS first starts to move in a westerly direction at a moderately slow speed. As the storm is fed by moist tropical air, it develops and increases speed, curving more in a north-westerly direction in the northern hemisphere and in a south-westerly direction in the southern hemisphere.

When it reaches its greatest intensity, with winds usually around 170-200 knots and the centre moving across the ocean surface at around 10-20 knots, it usually curves more towards the north or south in the northern and southern hemispheres respectively, finally curving away towards the eastern quadrant as it reaches higher latitudes, slowing and filling to eventually become a deep, but normal depression.

When a TRS strikes land it usually disintegrates as the moist sea air required to feed it is no longer available. However, in striking the land it can cause phenomenal damage, as witness the devastation caused by Cyclone Tracy in 1974 when winds of more than 300 kilometres per hour destroyed or damaged 90 per cent of the buildings in Darwin and killed more than sixty people.

Seasons

Climatic conditions suitable to the formation of a TRS only exist at certain times of the year, and although it is always possible to encounter a 'rogue' storm outside their seasons, for the most part these tropical disturbances can be predicted to occur within a few months of the year. Table 2 shows the *approximate* seasons for both northern and southern hemispheres and the main locations where tropical revolving storms occur:

Table 2 *Seasonal occurrence of tropical revolving storms*

Type	Season	Location
Hurricanes	July-November	North Atlantic (mostly western side)
Typhoons	July-November	North Pacific (western side)
Cyclones	June-November	Bay of Bengal, Arabian Sea
	November-April	South Pacific (western side), Timor Sea, South Indian Ocean (eastern side)

Radio warnings

Because of the extreme danger associated with TRSs, their development and movement is monitored closely. Special organisations are established to detect the birth of a TRS and broadcast warnings to all shipping and aircraft that might be in the area. These organisations go under different titles such as 'Cyclone Watch', 'Hurricane Watch' and the like, but all have a common purpose: to provide ample warning of the approach of tropical storm conditions. During the seasons, a twenty-four-hour watch is maintained on climatic conditions that are likely to give rise to a TRS, and to detect its presence at birth. From that moment on, all available facilities are engaged to monitor the movement of the storm and warn vessels that might lie within its reach.

Since the chances of riding out a TRS in a yacht or motor yacht are virtually non-existent, it would be a suicidal skipper who would put out for an extensive open-sea passage in tropical waters during the TRS season. However, these storms can be as dangerous in sheltered waters-even in harbours-as in the open sea, so any vessel of any size in such waters during the storm season, should post a permanent radio watch to listen for broadcast warnings. Moving at perhaps 25 knots, it does not take long for a cyclone or hurricane to run down an unprepared vessel, catching it even a few miles out from the coast with devastating results.

The radio warnings vary from country to country, but basically they are graded from simple cyclone (hurricane, typhoon) warnings to full scale red alerts as the storm is about to strike. A yacht receiving an initial stand-by warning that a TRS is developing within 500 miles or so, should immediately head for shelter. In tropical waters, many coastlines have anchorages that are specified as 'cyclone safe', although if the storm passes close, there is often no such thing as a cyclone safe anchorage. However, the important factor is that on receipt of the first warning, all boats in open water should put into the safest nearby harbour.

As the storm approaches, the warnings are upgraded. A boat caught out at sea with nowhere to go at this stage is in a desperate situation. In a cyclone that struck the Australian coast in the early 1900s, some thirty seagoing fishing vessels anchored in what was thought to be a secure cove, were dashed ashore with enormous loss of life. One boat was found several kilometres inland from the coast.

The severity and unpredictablility of a TRS must never be underestimated. The fact that it is not heading in your direction is no guarantee of safety; within hours it can alter its predicted track and suddenly be on your doorstep. Radio broadcasts must be monitored from the first preliminary warning until the final all-clear is given. It goes without saying that every boat sailing in tropical waters at this time of year should have a complete update on radio frequencies used for TRS warnings, and the procedures followed.

Visual warnings

Of course, it can always happen that for any number of reasons a yacht may find herself in tropical waters without the ability to receive radio TRS warnings. This is not a pleasant situation to be in, but since it could happen, it is important to know the visual signs that indicate the presence of a tropical storm and the action to take when the location and path of the storm are determined. Fortunately, the approach of a TRS is usually clearly indicated by physical signs, mostly in the sky or on the ocean. The main visual indicators are as follows:

1.   The barometer drops markedly. This is not just a significant drop in pressure, but, as the old salts used to put it, 'the bottom drops out of the barometer!'
2.   A low, but significant, swell begins to build up from the direction in which the storm is located. This may be felt up to 1000 kilometres from the storm centre. It is mostly noticeable because it may come from a different direction to the previous or prevailing swell.
3.   Distinctive cloud patterns appear across the sky, usually cirrus in bands radiating from a central point followed by an increasingly dense cloud cover. This increases as the storm approaches until the sky becomes totally black. The effect is rather like that of the approach of a severe cold front, magnified many times.
4.   An oppressive, heavy atmosphere settles around the boat, humidity is high and the air has a feeling of tension about it. Heavy rain begins to fall and the wind will make itself known for the first time.
5.   The wind picks up and changes direction from its previous (trade wind)

AUSTRALIAN ANTARCTIC DIVISION

bearing. As it increases in strength it takes on a 'banshee'-like howl, quite unmistakeable and chilling.

6.   As the storm approaches the wind will shift direction more and more rapidly as well as increasing in force.

The streaked surface of waves driven by cyclonic strength winds.

The centre of the storm

While surviving a cyclone (or hurricane, or typhoon) at sea in a small boat is an unlikely scenario, any vessel that finds herself in this unfortunate situation must take immediate steps to avoid the worst of the storm. The first step is to establish the position of the storm centre in relation to the boat's position, so that a plan can be devised to head away from the centre and minimise the effect. Since the storm is known to follow a fairly set path it is important to get as far away from that path as possible, and plotting the centre of the storm will help achieve this. The procedure is as follows:

1.   Face directly into the wind.

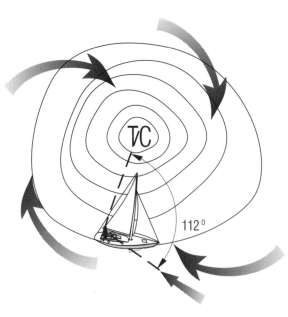

2.   The centre of the storm lies 10 points (112 degrees) to the left (southern hemisphere) or right (northern hemisphere).

3.   On the chart, plot the probable location of the storm and its expected path, as described earlier.

4.   Determine the most effective track out of the path of the storm, bearing in mind its tendency to curve as it enters higher latitudes.

Avoiding the storm

At this point, assuming that there is no way of getting out of the storm altogether, the procedure must be to take steps to avoid the worst. To do this, it is necessary to analyse the storm's move-

The centre of the storm lies 10 points (112 degrees) to the left when facing the wind (southern hemisphere) or right (northern hemisphere).

ments and the effect this might have on a boat caught within its path. For this purpose the storm is divided into two halves diametrically across its path; the front half of the storm is called the 'dangerous semi-circle' as this is the area where the most dangerous conditions are found.

If the boat lies in the path of the TRS or anywhere within the dangerous semi-circle, the storm is approaching either directly or indirectly and the skipper must take drastic action to get away by the most direct track or his craft will be literally swallowed up. By plotting the estimated position and path of the storm and the boat's position, the best means of getting the boat away from the storm will become apparent. Bearing in mind the speed of the storm itself and the fact that it follows a curving track, it should be possible, if not to get out of the dangerous semi-circle, then at least to reduce the danger by heading the boat away from the approaching centre.

Since heaving to or lying ahull are static methods of riding out a storm, neither will take the boat away from the approaching storm centre. The only procedure that will prove effective is to run before the wind, as described in Chapter 9. From the plot of the storm and the boat's position, a course can be set to enable the boat to run before or at least on a quartering wind away from the storm path. This not only points her in the right direction, it also gives her maximum sailing speed; a very necessary requirement at a time like this!

When making this plot, however, it must be kept in mind that the wind will shift as the storm closes (no boat can outrun a TRS). The planned sailing track out

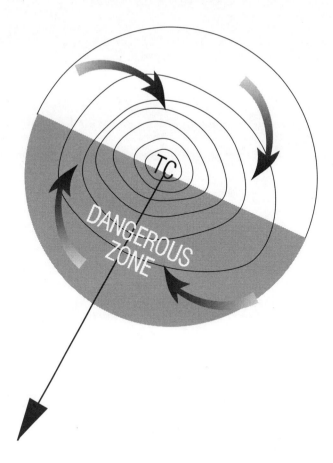

Boats caught in the path of the cyclones will need to move quickly away if they are to avoid the dangerous zone, which is formed by the front semicircle of the storm.

of the path of the storm must be made so that future wind shifts will not at a later stage 'head' the boat or hamper her fast run towards safety.

At the risk of becoming repetitive, it cannot be emphasised strongly enough that, in the first place, no yacht or small craft should be in open waters, far from shelter in the TRS season. And all boats, even those close inshore should maintain a twenty-four-hour watch on the radio broadcasts which are scheduled at this time of year solely to warn of the development and approach of a tropical storm. In all cases of carelessness at sea, the outcome can be terminal, but never more so that with tropical revolving storms.

CHAPTER 7

Preparing for a blow

As described in earlier chapters, most storms give plenty of notice that they are coming. Chapter 5 describes the various means of detecting the onset of a blow, including long-range forecasting by means of radio warnings, weatherfax read-outs, synoptic charts and other sophisticated methods, or short-term forecasting through local meteorological reports and visual sky signs.

Some 'nasty' weather systems such as tornadoes, willy-willies and turbulent cold fronts can move in fairly quickly, yet even these usually give notice of their arrival, albeit without much warning. But these are the exception, and as a rule the onset of bad weather is predictable, well ahead of its arrival, and moves in fairly slowly. Particularly is this the case in open waters where there are no local disturbances such as the close vicinity of land to upset the general weather pattern. While the sudden arrival of a turbulent system is always on the cards anywhere inshore or offshore, it is less likely to strike unexpectedly in the open ocean well away from landmasses.

Cold fronts, tornadoes, willy-willies and the like may move in quickly but also move out equally quickly. Pressure systems are never a problem for they take a while to build up. Low-pressure systems, the main harbingers of gales and storms, are never very fast moving unless they deepen to form tropical cyclones. Eeven then they give ample warning of their approach.

The boy scout motto

Generally speaking, a yacht caught at sea with an approaching storm usually has plenty of time to prepare for what might be coming. This time should be spent carefully preparing the boat and the crew for the worst, even though the indications may be of a moderate blow. While this may seem over-reacting in many cases, the old boy scout motto of being prepared is one that has also applied to seafarers since time immemorial. Whatever may eventuate in the ensuing few days, if the boat is correctly prepared, the crew need have no fears, for a sound and seaworthy boat is their best guarantee that they will come through safely.

By the same token, one small oversight in the preparation stage can create big problems later. The middle of a howling gale is no place to discover that a hatch was inadvertently left unlocked or an anchor not secured. Too late then to think of the window baffles that should have been in place or the sea anchor that should have been brought up and set up.

A check list is favoured by many experienced seamen, for it is easy to miss some small item in the anxiety of preparing for a blow, yet that item could make a great deal of difference to the ability of the boat to ride out the storm safely. Such a check list for preparing the boat and battening down is given in Chapter 8 and this should be followed in full, although, of course, adjustments will be required for individual craft. But this list can serve as a basis for individual lists, providing a check of procedures for battening down prior to a gale moving in.

Onset of a blow

As mentioned, most storms at sea move in fairly slowly and with plenty of warning. The sky signs indicating the approach and sometimes the character of the storm are described in Chapter 5. Short, savage blows, such as those induced by a cold front are soon over and do not usually build up much in the way of a sea. Wind waves may develop to a good sized chop, but it takes some time for a big swell to develop and unless the front is followed by consistent strong winds, the chances are that nothing more than a steep chop will develop. This type of condition will not concern an ocean-going vessel.

Most storms that are likely to build big seas and gale-force winds move in fairly slowly and are indicated some time before they arrive on the synoptic chart or in weather bulletins broadcast from shore stations. Some skippers may reduce sail as part of the pre-blow preparations, others prefer not to reef until the pressure of wind builds. Much depends on the type and rig of the boat and the experience of skipper and crew.

Offshore

If the boat is well out to sea there is little more to do once the boat has been prepared than sit and wait for the storm to move in. In borrowing yet again the boy scouts' motto, one aspect of being prepared for the worst is to get together food and drink for 'the duration'. If the storm turns out to be a particularly savage one,

or runs for longer than expected, it may be impossible to use the galley to cook food or heat drinks, and there is nothing more guaranteed to keep a crew's spirits boosted than hot coffee or soup and an occasional nourishing meal.

High Cirrus(mare's tails). Often the harbinger of an approaching frontal system.

While things are still normal, a couple of thermoses can be filled and sandwiches made and sealed in food wrap. Many a crew person, after two or three days of damp and discomfort, has blessed the cook who prepared solid sustenance beforehand. A small point before the event, but a lifesaver when all hell cuts loose!

This is mentioned in the check list together with other small but important, thoughtful items like ensuring a supply of dry clothes, but it is perhaps worth the extra mention here, for food and hot drinks in any climate, but particularly in cold climates, can make a big difference to the way a crew rides out a severe storm.

Inshore

Obviously there will be little difference in a check list for riding out a storm at sea or in waters close to a coastline. But there is one factor which applies to inshore waters that is not present in the preparation of boats well out to sea. That is the

101

Fair weather cumulus. Nothing to worry about with this sky condition.

possibility of running for shelter rather than staying out and riding out the storm in the open sea.

There are many schools of thought on this, and it is important to examine the various factors, because while a run in to shelter in a bay or harbour may provide a comfortable, safe way of riding out the storm, it can equally be the most disastrous move the boat could make and result in the loss of both the boat and her crew. There is no hard and fast rule because, assuming the boat is seaworthy and capable of staying out at sea, much depends on the coastline, what shelter it offers and what access there is to that shelter.

If the boat is not capable of riding it out — small boats caught out fishing or sailing in open waters, for example — then there is no choice but to run back in to shelter, regardless of the risks. But with seaworthy vessels such as yachts or large powered craft, the hazards can often be greater heading inshore to shelter than staying out in the open water. There is nothing more comfortable than listening to the howling of a full-blown gale while snugged up to an anchor in some sheltered anchorage, so the temptation is always there. But before succumbing to that temptation, the pros and cons must be carefully examined and the safest option taken.

102

If shelter lies in a river or harbour with a barred entrance, then the chances are it would be safer to stay out at sea. As the waves build, they develop a much more ferocious configuration close to a coast, with the swells ricocheting back off cliffs or breakwaters and creating unpleasant and dangerous sea conditions. Similarly, a strong run-out of tide can create equally dangerous steep seas in the entrance, some of which can overwhelm even solid, seaworthy vessels. In the late 1970s, a British yachtsman approaching the coast of Australia after sailing around the world from the United Kingdom was lost, together with his yacht, while trying to make into a port in a moderate blow. Having survived months of open ocean and hundreds of ports, his anxiety to make into port overcame his prudence, and he was claimed by a particularly savage bar condition.

Even open bays, where there is easy access, must be carefully assessed before seeking shelter in their seemingly protective waters. How much sea room is there if the wind changes direction or the anchor drags? Has the bay a good holding bottom? Big swells swinging the boat around can soon pluck out even a well-secured anchor, and with a full-blown gale in progress the last place to be dragging anchor or trying to get sails up is close to a coast. There is no room here for lying ahull or using a sea anchor, or any of the other standard techniques used in riding out a blow. A boat caught close to the coast has to get out of there as quickly as she can and by whatever means she can.

So it is very important, when considering a run for shelter, to analyse the situation closely and ensure that if you take your boat inshore, no change of conditions will subsequently put her in danger. As a general rule, most experienced seaman choose to head out to sea rather than close with the coast when a blow is in the offing. And this, perhaps better than any expert advice, sums up the situation completely.

CHAPTER 8

A pre-gale check list

Most experienced skippers have a check list to cover the routine procedures of preparing for a blow. While all vessels are different, a basic check list would probably read something like this:

- Close all ventilators and seal all openings.
- Close all sea cocks.
- Secure hatches, if needs be with strong backs.
- Cover large windows or ports with baffles.
- Secure all anchors and deck gear.
- Check rigging for any signs of wear or damage.
- Check spreaders and spars for wear or damage.
- Tie down any loose ropes.
- Check life-jackets and place handy to the companionway.
- Check deck harnesses and place handy.
- Run motor to top up batteries, check fuel.
- Check all loose gear in the cabin is tied down.
- Ditto in galley area.
- Take out and check emergency steering gear.
- If used, rig cockpit dodger.
- Check all safety and emergency gear including EPIRB (emergency position-indicating radio beacon).
- Establish radio contact with shore station, if possible, and advise of the situation.
- Plot the boat's position and determine proximity of any dangers, particular islands, reefs, lee shores.
- Make sandwiches and thermoses of hot drinks.
- Switch off the gas at the bottle.
- Prepare storm sails and running gear.
- Check lights, especially spreader lights Prepare emergency lighting such as candles, torches.

- Rig life-lines along the deck.
- Check life-raft, contents and release gear.
- Check life-ring and dan buoy plus release gear and lights.
- Rig lee cloths on bunks.
- Prepare wet-weather clothing, with changes.
- Check and prepare sea anchor and oil bag, warps.
- Check extra warps for streaming astern.
- Check reefing gear and prepare.
- Check that pulpit, stanchions and life-lines are secure.
- Rig nets if required.
- Place knife, axe, other emergency gear in cockpit.
- Check pumps and pump bilges.
- Place buckets in handy location.
- Put changes of dry clothing in plastic bags.
- Check signalling gear, flares and rockets.

It is important to understand the need for each item on the check list and the danger that can result from not completing a thorough check. Carrying out such checks in the 'calm before the storm' is a relatively simple procedure compared to trying to close a hatch that has blown open and strained its hinges, or worse, trying to secure a rampaging anchor that is charging around the deck at the height of the storm. Such actions involve considerable risk to both life, limb and the boat.

If ever there was a practical application of the proverbial stitch in time, it is in securing the boat for a blow. A few minutes effort before the storm arrives can avoid life-threatening problems when it has moved in.

Close all ventilators

Although many ventilators are designed to shed water and allow air into the cabin, they are intended mostly for operation in normal sailing conditions when the water that comes aboard is mostly spray. Few can withstand the onslaught of a boarding wave thundering with considerable impact into the ventilator opening. Some water is almost certain to get below and it only takes a cupful in the electronics to render the radio useless, thus cutting the boat off completely from communication with the outside world.

Radar, satnav, depth sounders and all other electronic gear can follow suit with disastrous results. Water in the bilges can slosh around and affect engine electrics, creating yet another problem at a time when problems are the last thing in the world you want. Even the smallest amount of water in the cabin can create at least discomfort, at worst disaster.

The need to close off the ventilators is obvious, then, and most experienced skippers will not rest at just closing them off, but will cover and seal them with bungs and/or waterproof covers. Some older types might need to be removed and the hole in the deckhead plugged and sealed.

Close sea-cocks

The danger here comes from the possibility of a pipe rupturing or a pipe clip coming undone and flooding the bilges. It is not unknown for this to happen with the boat moving around violently in a seaway. Sometimes fittings, such as toilets, move and create stress on intake or discharge pipes. This is perhaps not a major problem since if it happens, the sea cock can be quickly shut to stop the flow of the water into the boat, but by the time it is discovered, enough water can flood into the boat to cause discomfort, even danger, so it is wise to have all sea cocks closed beforehand.

Ventilators like this can cope with spray and other boarding water in moderate conditions but must be plugged or covered when the going gets tough.

Secure hatches

The largest opening in the hull structure occurs at a hatch (or doorway, which is technically a hatch) and the amount of water allowed into the hull through such an opening will create immediate and serious problems. In the middle of a blow, green seas will be boarding and rolling down the decks. Any opening at all will create problems; an open hatch will be the first step to disaster.

We have seen how a small amount of water can be dangerous inside the hull; the quantity that will flood in through an open hatch will create havoc, damaging electronic and electrical equipment and saturating everything else. Sufficient water in the hull will make the boat sluggish and unresponsive, so that she will not rise to oncoming seas, and more and more water will pour aboard. This is the thin edge of a very terminal wedge!

107

Hatches are always vulnerable and must be strengthened or covered if sea conditions are likely to deteriorate.

Securing the hatches with their own fittings is usually sufficient, but some catches are notoriously weak and the hatch can be ripped open by the impact of a boarding sea. Because of the extreme danger of losing a hatch in a seaway, many experienced skippers double up on the normal hatch fastenings by using a strong back across the coaming. This is a good-sized length of timber or metal, placed across the underside of the hatch coaming and secured to the hatch by means of rope or turnbuckles or some other fastening device. This removes any risk of the hatch being torn off, since it would also involve tearing off the hatch coaming, and this is an integral part of the deck construction. This is, of course, not the only method of ensuring the security of a hatch, but it is one of the oldest, one of the simplest and one of the most effective.

Cover windows

Motor yachts or cruisers and sailboats with large windows in their cabin coachhouse may need to be protected against these windows being stove in by a sea. Portholes are usually too small to be vulnerable and in any case have scuttles which can be lowered over them. But large windows are very vulnerable and the impact of a boarding sea can smash them in, leaving a large opening through which other seas will follow, with the results described earlier.

Covering windows is usually just a question of placing previously made timber baffles or screens over them. Providing they are well secured so that they cannot be swept off by the boarding seas, these baffles can be fairly basic, consisting of just a few planks or boards fastened together on a frame to completely cover the windows. There are many different methods of keeping them in place, the only requirement being that they can withstand the impact of a boarding sea.

Secure anchors

Many vessels carry their anchors on deck or in fittings close to the bow. They are generally well secured when the boat is at sea, but often need extra lashing when a storm is approaching. An anchor that breaks away in the middle of a gale is akin to a wild bull escaping from its stockyard; it can do an awful lot of damage before it is restrained and secured again. At best it-the anchor-will charge around, damaging the deck, possibly windows and fittings. At worst it can flop over the side and puncture the hull.

All anchors stowed on deck must be securely lashed, then double lashed before the onset of the blow, and any patent fittings holding them in place must be checked and doubled up with a lashing if needs be. Anchors stowed below must also be well secured for they can do as much damage charging around inside the hull as they can on deck. The warp should also be well secured or it may be lost over the side and create handling problems if it wraps around the rudder or propeller.

A convenient place to carry the anchor under normal conditions, but it must be securely lashed before the boats gets into a seaway.

Check rigging

If there is one thing you do not need in the middle of riding out a gale, it is something going wrong with the rigging. There will be obvious problems if the standing rigging gives way-the loss of the mast being one. But even running rigging that is damaged or deteriorating can provide unwanted headaches at a time when climbing the mast is just not on.

It's easy to go aloft in sailing vessels of this size, but checking the rigging at sea in a yacht is not so easy.

Usually a quick check of the rigging is all that is needed; apart from the uppermost stays, any whiskering or similar problems with the standing rigging will be visible from deck level. If a shroud or stay is suspect, it would be worthwhile placing a doubler on it just in case it parts at an awkward time. A halyard running from the top of the mast and winched tight onto the chainplates is a good stand-by for doubtful shrouds or stays, and should be effective enough to hold the mast in place until the weather moderates and the problem can be resolved.

Running rigging is more likely to be in need of attention than standing rigging, especially where it runs over sheaves or blocks. The sheaves themselves may wear and jam, or the aluminium mast wall surrounding the sheave may wear and allow the halyard to slip off the sheave. Either way, if the problem is at the mast cap, fixing it is going to be very difficult at any time, but no more so than during a blow. Best to check these items before the boat leaves the dock, and then double check prior to riding out the gale. A jamming halyard during an emergency hoisting of a sail can lead to a catastrophe.

Check spreaders and spars

The spreaders, or crosstrees, are the weakest point in the rigging of many yachts and since the spreaders will come under enormous strain when the boat is rolling around in a big seaway, even without sails, a check is essential for peace of mind, if not to avoid losing the mast.

This may involve a trip up in the bosun's chair, but as a general rule any serious weakness will mostly be seen from the deck. Moving the cap shrouds will sometimes indicate any damage or give warning of any potential failure in the metal in the spreaders. Particularly note the condition of spreader fittings, since corrosion between the mast wall and the metal fittings can cause problems in this area.

Spars, such as the boom, should also come in for scrutiny, even though they are close to the deck and within reach. The old maxim of it being easier to fix

things while it is all quiet is one that applies to this, as well as other aspects of checking the gear before the onset of the blow.

Loose ropes

There is never a time on board a boat when loose ropes are not a hazard. Power or sail, a loose rope is a menace because it can foul with almost anything and cause problems that can sometimes prove serious. Everyone knows the problems of ropes around propellers or rudders, and every sailor worth his salt will know of the hazards of loose ropes aloft, jamming or tangling gear at times when untangling can be both risky and a nuisance.

When the boat is caught in a severe blow and it is dangerous to go out on deck, leave alone climb up the rigging or scrabble over the side, then a loose rope can be life-threatening. Nothing is more likely to create a terminal situation than a fouled propeller or tangled rigging at a time when a crisis is looming and the engine or a sail is needed to get out of it. Many a distressed vessel has had its distress exacerbated by a loose rope in the wrong place at the wrong time, and there would probably not be a seaman afloat who has not, at some time or another, cursed the normally useful length of braided or laid synthetic for doing what it was not designed to do.

Yet the most likely time for rope to become loose and cause problems is when the boat is riding out a gale. Prevention is better than cure, they say, and since the cure is extremely difficult in this case, prevention is the only way to avoid the problem. Prior to the onset of the blow, one of the important items on the check list must be to stow away all rope that is not actually in use and secure any that cannot be stowed. Obvious items such as life-lines will be well secured of necessity, but ropes not in use, such as halyards and sheets, lifebuoy lines and any spare lines kept at hand for emergency use, must be checked to ensure that they are well coiled and secured so they will not come undone, even when big seas roar along the deck.

Life-lines

These are definitely not loose pieces of rope. On the contrary, they cannot be secured too well. Life-lines are stout ropes run along the deck to provide handholds and harness attachments for crew that might have to carry out work on deck. It goes without saying that leaving the cockpit at the height of a gale is a perilous move, but sometimes it has to be done. The normal handrails may be adequate, although often there are gaps between such rails and the next secure point. Then the life-lines, which are stretched tight along the deck at a reasonable working height, provide something secure to hang onto.

Similarly with harness clips. There may not always be a convenient stay or rail onto which to clip the harness line. In this case the life-line provides a securing point at any stage along the deck and allows good freedom of movement while working in a harness. These lines must obviously be strong enough to withstand considerable weight and attached to the boat very securely as they may, and quite possibly will, mean the difference between life and death for crew if an emergency arises. They need to be prepared and placed in position long before the blow moves in.

Storm sails and gear

Safety harnesses are a must at all times on the open ocean, and never moreso that when the boat is riding out a storm.

There is no telling beforehand just how strong the winds may be. A well-found, sizeable yacht may be able to carry basic storm rig throughout even a severe gale. And if sail can be carried, then it should be used, for not only does it make life more comfortable aboard, but it also keeps the boat under better control. Even if the boat will eventually have to ride it out under bare poles, the use of storm sails will ensure than she can be kept moving as long as possible under the best possible conditions.

Most storm suits consist of a spitfire jib and loose-footed tri-sail, although some skippers prefer just the spitfire jib, much depending on how the boat balances and performs under reduced rig. Whatever the choice, the period prior to the onset of the blow is the time to get the storm suit out and check it through, ensuring that all the required fittings are attached and the sails are ready for hoisting when needed. A check of the sail itself, in terms of stitching and wear, should have been made before; the twenty-four hours prior to a blow is no time to be repairing a storm sail!

Similarly, running rigging for the storm sails should be checked and placed in readiness. The halyards will probably be those already in use with normal sails,

113

but the sheets and blocks may well be specific to the storm gear, and these must be checked to see that they are not only rigged, but are in good condition.

Reefing gear

Like the storm sails and fittings, the reefing gear is also likely to come in for some use, and should be checked beforehand to ensure that when it is required it operates smoothly and effectively. Particularly is this the case with 'jiffy' reefing, where it may be necessary to check that the various fittings are in place. In the middle of a blow with the sails half reefed is no time to discover that a vital shackle or hook is missing. This preparation period is also a good time to check that the crew are familiar with the reefing procedures.

Furling or roller reefing gear is relatively easy to check, as is slab reefing, but a run-through with the crew prior to the onset of the storm is always a wise practice and avoids heartburn and recrimination, to say nothing of possible injury, when the work has to be done under adverse conditions. This is no place to go into detail on the bits and piece of the various reefing gear as it comes in many shapes and many forms; suffice it to say that whatever the gear, the crew should be familiar with its operation.

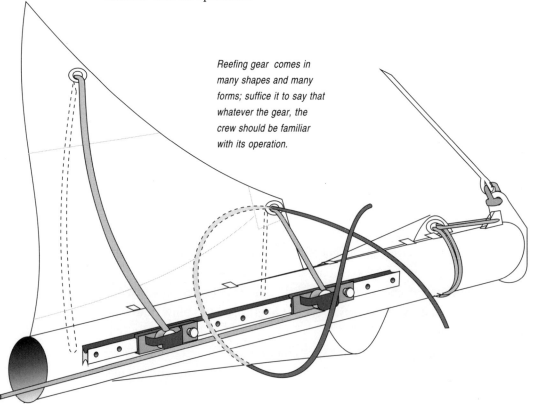

Reefing gear comes in many shapes and many forms; suffice it to say that whatever the gear, the crew should be familiar with its operation.

Pulpit and rails

On smaller yachts particularly, the pulpit and stanchions that secure the life-rails may not be sufficiently strong to withstand heavy impact; the sort of impact that can occur when one of the crew, caught off balance, is thrown heavily. Loose or rusted deck bolts can create such situations that may not be seen in the normal course of sailing, but can prove disastrous in a heavy seaway.

While it is too late to make major repairs just as the storm is moving in, at least if the danger is known it can be covered by a temporary repair or, at worst, the crew can be warned of the possible danger. A harness secured to a pulpit rail could prove fatal if the rail gave way when the weight of a body came onto it. Checking around the rails and stanchions beforehand can avoid such situations. One experienced ocean-going skipper likes to test his rails by securing the harness to them and jumping over the side to simulate the sort of stress that could be encountered in a big sea. This is not recommended as a general practice!

There are a number of other items of equipment which some experienced ocean-going sailors like to have in place before moving into a storm situation, but these vary greatly with the type of boat and the composition of the crew. For example, if there are small children aboard, a wise move is to rig safety nets inside the rails. While small children should not be on deck during a blow, factors such as claustrophobia or seasickness can make it necessary for them to leave the cabin. Even the cockpit is not safe under severe conditions, so the netting provides a bonus safety measure just in case. Indeed, most boats with children on board have the netting in place in fine weather as well as in foul.

The life-raft

This check should be automatic. As potentially the most important piece of safety equipment on the boat, the life-raft should come in for regular checking anyway, and be double checked before a blow sets in. Apart from the normal routine examination, the lashings must be carefully examined at this time to ensure that the raft does not come adrift if struck by a boarding sea. Extra lashings may be necessary, but these, if used, must be so secured that the raft can be released quickly in an emergency.

A typical liferaft for small vessels. The lashings should be thoroughly checked before the onset of a blow.

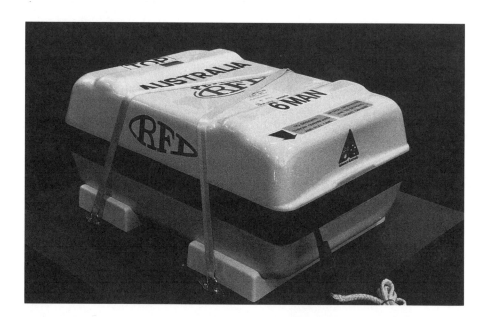

Life-rings and deck safety gear

Deck safety gear varies from boat to boat and individual to individual, but all seagoing craft should carry life-rings with dan buoys and lights. These must be carefully examined in the pre-blow check because if one of the crew is lost overboard-a very possible happening in storm conditions-his or her life may depend on the quick release and effectiveness of this equipment.

As with the life-raft, extra lashings may be necessary to prevent the gear being washed away when big seas pour across the decks, but by the same token such lashings must not hinder any quick release of any part of the gear if it is required. Dan buoys are particularly vulnerable because of their size, but again, these can mean the difference between life and death to a person in the water, so they must be secured in such a way that they can be quickly and easily released.

Automatic life-ring lights can usually be tested, but self-igniting flares can only be examined externally to see that they are in apparently good working order. Any other safety equipment kept on deck should also be checked, bearing in mind the comment made earlier in this check list about ropes and lines.

Spray dodgers can be useful

Since at least one member of the crew is likely to be permanently located in the cockpit, handling the helm, some sort of shelter is necessary to protect him or her from the worst of the weather conditions. If the boat has an adequate doghouse, the problem does not arise, but without something to break the fury of the wind and spray, the helmsman may soon become exhausted, perhaps numbed and certainly saturated. Although not providing complete shelter, a canvas dodger takes the worst out of the weather and is a standard fitting on most ocean-going craft with open cockpits.

Some skippers leave the dodger permanently in place, in which case it needs only to be raised and secured to prepare for a blow. If it is kept stowed below, then it is another item that must be attended to before the storm begins and thus forms an important item on the check list.

The fastening of hatches and portholes has already been dealt with, and the companionway should be given priority when this is done. Access to the cabin

Canvas (or synthetic) spray dodgers can be a godsend at sea, providing shelter from all sorts of unpleasant conditions.

from the cockpit is essential unless the storm develops to the point where the boat is battened down completely, but great care must be taken in using that access, for if a sea crashes aboard at a moment when the companionway door or weatherboards are open, it will pour below with potentially disastrous results. A dodger can help to prevent this.

Where weatherboards are used, a good precaution is to leave the bottom boards in place and climb over them to get below. The aperture must be closed again as soon as possible, but this procedure does ensure that if a sea boards when someone is entering or leaving the cabin, the water will mostly be kept in the cockpit, where is will cause no problems. Opening a companionway door or taking out all the weatherboards invites a boarding sea to flood the cabin below. Great care is needed here.

Emergency gear

With most of the deck gear checked out, attention now turns to the cabin, where the first and most important items to be checked are the various pieces of safety equipment. These, of course, include life-jackets, which should be unearthed from stowage, and laid out handy for use if needed; likewise, the safety harnesses, which should be placed convenient to the companionway. In a heavy blow, no person should leave the cabin without first donning a harness.

Various items of emergency gear such as flares, rockets and the like should all be checked and placed where they can be easily reached if necessary, and the EPIRBs (emergency position-indicating radio beacons) tested by means of their check buttons. An axe, a knife and various other bits and pieces should be placed close to the companionway so they can be reached from deck if needed in a hurry to clear away fallen rigging and ropes.

First aid kit, buckets; the list is endless, but all should be checked and placed in a convenient spot against the possibility of an emergency arising. It is too late, when the emergency has arrived, to go fumbling around in a pitch dark, gyrating cabin looking for some desperately needed piece of safety gear. It must all be checked and placed handy long before there is any likelihood of it being needed. Experienced skippers know this and take great pains to draw up extensive check lists for use prior to riding out a storm.

A useful and necessary item that should come in for attention at this stage is the 'abandon ship' bag. It may not be a bag, of course, it may be a box or any other, preferably watertight, container. It contains the emergency supplies of food and equipment that will be needed in the life-raft should the worst happen and the

118

crew has to abandon ship. It cannot be placed in the life-raft prior to inflation, so it is kept handy to the companionway and when the raft is inflated the emergency container can be tossed into it. Like most other emergency gear, this container will be stowed away in some secure spot for most of the passage, but prior to riding out a blow, it must be brought out, checked and placed in handy position.

A basic rule usually enforced on most boats is to turn off the gas at the bottle in case the wild plunging of the boat in the seas causes a fracture of the gas pipe or stress on a fitting. Either way, leaking gas can create extreme danger in the cabin and shutting off the cock at the bottle is the only way to avoid this.

Another important item of emergency gear which may well be needed is the sea anchor. This is usually well stowed away at the bottom of a locker, but must now be unearthed and checked out. Similarly, the oil bag, if used, a supply of fish oil and the warp must be readied and placed where they can be easily reached if required. Spare warps for streaming astern can be prepared at the same time, for they are generally stowed together in the same locker.

Emergency lighting is an important factor on the check list. Torches, matches, lanterns and/or candles should be prepared in case battery power is lost during the storm. Fumbling around in the dark during an emergency is a sure way to invite trouble and although torches are the ideal emergency equipment in this situation, batteries can quickly become exhausted when used constantly. Candles are not usually very effective in the gyrating cabin of a boat riding out a storm, but lanterns are ideal and can often be used on deck as well, if the need arises.

While on the subject of lighting, a quick check round the boat's electrics at this time is a wise procedure; failure of the navigation lights can be unpleasant, especially if the boat is in or near any shipping lanes, and work on deck is made much easier and safer if the spreader lights are working. Over and above the lights, of course, is the need for electric power to operate the various instruments, notably radio, satellite navigator and radar. So a check of the electric system, particularly the batteries, is very much in order as part of the check list.

Securing below decks

Much of the below-deck check list consists of fairly obvious routines such as placing lee cloths on the bunks, securing all items likely to be thrown in the event of heavy pounding or rolling and securing the galley. As mentioned earlier, it is generally wise to turn off the gas at the bottle before the blow really gets under way, and since this means the galley will be out of action for the duration, everything in or around it should be stowed away or well secured.

Cupboards and lockers that have light closing devices should be locked or otherwise fixed so that they cannot fly open if their contents start charging around. Anything which is suspect or cannot be secured in place should be removed to the cabin sole.

At this point in time it is a good move to run the motor and charge up the batteries. They can be checked with a hydrometer and topped up with distilled water if necessary so that maximum life is available when the storm commences. This can be done at the same time the electrics are tested so that there is still time for any quick running repairs if necessary.

Wet weather gear must be sorted out and placed handy, for the crew may well be living in this gear for some days. Baby napkins (*not* the disposable type!) are the best invention yet for preventing chafe and drying out wet body areas, and experienced sailors will always have a good supply on board. Dry clothing should be packed in plastic bags and stowed away in a convenient locker, for there is nothing more demoralising than living, sleeping and eating in wet clothes for days on end, and most gales last for at least a few days.

Final preparations

With the boat battened down and everything stowed or secured, there are a few final chores to finish before the boat and her crew are ready to batten down. These are usually left to the last minute when the blow has moved in and indicated that it is not going to just huff and puff a little then move away, it is going to develop into a full force 10 gale.

First move is to establish the boat's exact position on the chart and note the proximity of any hazards such as islands, reefs, coastlines, shipping lanes and the like. Navigation is important, but at this stage the only requirement is knowing where the boat is at the start of the blow and what is around her.

Radio contact with a shore station is next on the list; advise a shore-based operator of the developing scenario and request a watch be kept on a prearranged frequency at a prearranged time in case any emergencies should arise. If the boat is well out to sea and contact with shore cannot be established, then contact with shipping in the area is an alternative. It is important to make radio contact with someone before the gale sets in, for although every precaution may have been taken, even the best laid plans of mice and seamen can go astray at this time, and knowing someone is within listening range is a comforting thought.

Finally, it is always wise to prepare food and hot drinks before the galley is closed down so that the crew are not reduced to eating biscuits and drinking water. Hot soup, coffee or tea will hold its temperature for some time in a thermos, and in cold weather there is nothing more invigorating to an exhausted body, and nothing that restores the demoralised spirit more than a hot drink. Often it will be possible to use the galley, depending on how the boat is riding out the seas, but just in case the gas has to be turned off, a few thermoses should be filled as a wise stand-by.

Similarly with sandwiches. An hour or two spent making sandwiches beforehand can pay big dividends when a cold and hungry crew come below off a deck watch. Wrapped in plastic sealer film, sandwiches will keep fresh for some days, and once again, nothing is more guaranteed to restore flagging spirits or low morale, than full bellies. When all the other preparation on the check list have been carried out, a little domesticity in the galley will ensure that the boat and her crew are well prepared for anything the elements may throw at her.

CHAPTER 9

Riding it out

Hopefully, all the preparation will have been unnecessary and the storm will either disperse, disintegrate or pass away. If that happens, you can breathe the proverbial deep sight of relief, dismantle the emergency provisions and break out the champagne. But if the storm continues its approach, and you know that you are going to have to ride it out, then at least you can be reassured by the fact that you have taken every possible step to ensure the boat is ready for the onslaught.

Psychologically, you can prepare yourself as well, knowing that a well-found yacht is the safest vessel afloat, and while your next few hours, perhaps days, are not going to be the most comfortable of your life, the chances are they are not going to be the worst. If it is your first real blow, it would be totally natural that you are apprehensive, even scared; that's a feeling that will persist for quite a few stormy encounters to come. But while familiarity must never be allowed to breed contempt where storms at sea are concerned, it does develop confidence in the boat and reassurance that she is going to ride out anything the elements can throw at her.

Think it through. If the hull is sound (and if it's not then it shouldn't be out there in the first place) it will hold together through anything the sea may throw against it. That's what all the factors described in Chapter 1 are about; a sound hull will not disintegrate unless it is smashed onto something solid, like the shore. And you have already prepared for this by ensuring that you are well away from any coast. Nor will it develop dangerous leaks; you have prepared for this, too, by closing off and sealing any openings in the hull structure.

A yacht cannot capsize, at least, not if it is a monohull type with a properly ballasted keel. This is where the design factor comes into play, also described in Chapter 1. The ballast keel creates a righting lever that will come into effect whenever the boat heels, and no matter how far over she may roll in a big seas, she will bounce back upright. She can go right over-even complete a 360 degree roll-but still she *must* come back upright. Like those blow-up clowns in children's playgrounds; the more you push the boat over, the more the righting lever of the keel comes into play, and the more determined will be her recovery to the upright.

Certainly, if she rolls right over, you might lose the mast and above-deck gear, but that's relatively superficial and clearing the decks in this way is unlikely to place the boat in any immediate danger; providing, of course, that the structure

123

of the hull is not damaged in the process. Generally speaking, when this sort of capsize takes place it is only a matter of clearing away the debris so that it cannot puncture the hull, after which the boat will be sitting upright, afloat and, hopefully, with only broken crockery as the worst damage.

Later, we'll deal with the recovery from such situations, but at this stage, with the storm about to break and all preparations, both physical and mental in place, you need now to turn your attention on to your tactics for riding out the blow. Of course you can't at this stage know just how severe it's going to be, but as with the boy scout motto, the best approach is to prepare for the worst, and if the worst doesn't come, then you are well prepared for any lesser eventuality.

How to ride it out

There are a number of different ways of riding out a storm successfully. Apart from the traditional techniques, which are mostly related to monohull, ballasted vessels, there are many individual methods which have been developed through experience in different conditions with different types of craft. The techniques used for a multihull or centreboard yacht, for example, would obviously be quite different to those used with a ballast-keel yacht. Similarly, riding it out in a motor yacht requires a totally different approach again.

Because multihulls come in many and varied forms, and because centreboard yachts are not really designed for ocean crossing, attempting to cover the more specialised techniques that apply to these craft would not be feasible in a book such as this. However, riding out a blow in any vessel involves a number of fundamental factors, and it is these that form the basis of the techniques described here principally for use on traditional keel yachts.

The preparations for the onset of a blow were described in the previous chapter. You have prepared the boat physically and yourself mentally. Now the storm moves in. Comfort, relaxation and enjoyment must now take a back seat to survival. Secure in the knowledge that the boat is sound, you must now determine what tactics to employ, not only to ensure you survive the blow, but also to ensure that you do so in as comfortable a way as possible.

There are four main conventional methods of riding out a blow:

- heaving to
- lying ahull
- running before
- lying to a sea anchor

The choice of which to choose depends on a number of factors. Previous experience with the same yacht will immediate indicate which method should be adopted; rarely do two boats react the same way to riding out heavy seas, and previous experience with a particular boat is invaluable. The intensity of the storm will be a factor, as will the location of any nearby coastline or other hazard. The experience of the crew and skipper will also have a bearing, for in all these matters, one of the most important factors is experience.

Experience in handling the boat under storm conditions, experience in the ways of the sea when the giant waves build up and experience in how to reduce the stresses on the boat to a minimum. With such experience comes a cool head and calm actions; the secret of any form of survival, but none more so than in the open sea when things turn nasty. Also with such experience comes the knowledge of which method of riding it out best suits the boat and the prevailing conditions at the time.

Heaving to

This method involves the use of sails, so it is limited to situations where the wind strength still allows a certain amount of sail to be carried. Most experienced sailors would adopt this as the first step in riding out a blow, using it to hold the boat in a reasonably comfortable position before the wind strength increases to the point where it is not safe for the boat to carry canvas any more.

It is a technique often used outside storm conditions, even in quite moderate weather since it offers a method whereby the boat can be held in a near-stationary position, comfortably lying with her bow just off the wind and sea. There are often situations where such a manoeuvre is useful, notably while waiting to enter a harbour, or waiting for another boat at a predetermined rendezvous. But its most useful application is when the wind gets too strong to continue sailing comfortably and the boat needs to be put into a 'hold' situation, riding comfortably to wind and sea, yet making virtually no forward progress.

The manoeuvre involves simply backing one sail against another-the jib against the main (usually reefed at this stage). The wonderful old square-rigged sailing ships hove to frequently whenever they need to stay in one position for any length of time; picking up or dropping a pilot or transferring people from one ship to another. Their method involved backing the lower sails against the uppers; today's fore-and-aft rigged yachts follow the same basic procedure by backing the headsail against the main.

This has the effect of one sail cancelling out the other; the jib attempting to

Heaving to involves simply backing one sail against another- the jib against the main (usually reefed at this stage).

push the bow off the wind and the main trying to drive the bow up into the wind. As a result the driving forces of the sails cancel each other and the boat comes to a halt with her bow just off the wind. This situation can be 'locked in' so to speak, by putting the helm down, which, prevents her head from falling off the wind.

Since the wind and sea run in roughly the same direction, this means that the boat, when brought up, is also lying with her bow at an angle just off the seas-the most comfortably position for any boat to lie. Taking the seas at a modest angle to the bow avoids excessive rolling or pitching, panting or pounding. Because she is not secured to anything, the boat will naturally drift a little, but the heaving to situation minimises this drift, which is in a quarterly (down-wind) direction.

Providing the wind doesn't shift, the boat should remain locked into this position, riding comfortably at an angle to wind and sea. If she is not lying comfortably, the attitude can be adjusted by easing away on the main sheet, to allow her head to fall more off the wind. Bringing up the helm can achieve a similar effect. Because every boat has a different wetted area below the waterline, and therefore presents different lateral resistance to the water, a certain amount of adjustment will be required to find the setting of sails and helm to hold her in the most comfortable position.

To get into the heave to attitude from any sailing attitude, the yacht must be

126

first brought up close-hauled to the wind. The jib is then be backed by one of two methods: either physically dragging it across the other side of the bow against the wind; or tacking the boat without releasing the jib sheet. Either method will cause the jib to back against the wind and try to force the bow away. This is counteracted by sheeting on the main and putting the helm down, then adjusting both until the most comfortable position is found.

With all sheets and the helm secured in this position, the boat will gradually move into the static heaving to position. As mentioned, adjustments can be made by means of main sheet or helm until she is brought up at an angle to wind and sea, riding comfortably, virtually in the close-hauled position. Not only will the sails hold her in this position, but they will also reduce the rolling action of the hull by creating wind resistance as the mast gyrates across the sky.

Lying ahull

Unfortunately, heaving to is usually restricted to the early stages of a blow. When the wind increases to the point that the boat can no longer carry any sail, the choice of how to ride it out involves one of the three other methods, all of which are mainly carried out under bare poles. It goes without saying that a decision to abandon the heaving to method must be made before conditions deteriorate to such an extent that taking off the remaining sails will be too dangerous for the crew.

The simplest method of riding it out without sails, and the one favoured by many seasoned ocean-crossing skippers, is lying ahull. It is simple because it involves nothing more than lashing the helm and leaving the boat to her own devices. As described earlier, a well-found yacht is virtually indestructible, so she can be left to roll around, wallow, pitch and yaw as much as she chooses, her crew confident in the knowledge that her designer and builder prepared her for such torturous treatment. In this situation, the boat is nothing more than a bobbing cork; at the mercy of wind and wave, but with no risk that she will not cope more than competently with both, and bounce up at the end, as sound and safe as she was when the blow started.

But while the yacht will take it all in her stride, the skipper and crew will experience a nightmare ride not unlike, in some respects, going over Niagara Falls in a barrel! Anything more uncomfortable is hard to imagine, for in doing her own thing while riding out the storm, the boat will go through some heinous contortions; rolling, plunging and twisting through the seas, and creating a private hell within the enclosed capsule of her hull where the crew are confined.

127

Lying ahull is simple because it involves nothing more than lashing the helm and leaving the boat to her own devices.

Any semblance of comfort for the occupants will be a mere hallucination as they are thrown from one side of the cabin to another, often via the deckhead or floor. Utensils, books and anything else not screwed down will become airborne missiles as the interior of the yacht resembles the inside of a spaceship gone crazy. Add to this the claustrophobic, oppressive, sometimes fetid atmosphere inside the totally enclosed cabin and you will have some idea why this method is not popular with all experienced sailors.

In short, while lying ahull may be a safe and seamanlike way to ride out a storm, it is at the same time the most uncomfortable. Rolling to each wave and flopping from crest to trough exaggerates the normal action of the boat in a seaway. Lacking the steadying influence of the sails, and with the pendulum effect of the ballast keel amplifying each movement, the boat becomes a torture chamber for those enclosed in the cabin.

Seasickness and injury are very real possibilities in this situation, even for the most experienced and hardened ocean sailors, and these can also add to the misery. In some cases the violent motion can be modified by hoisting a small

128

steadying sail, but as a rule, when the situation has deteriorated to the point where lying ahull is necessary, the wind is too strong to carry any sail whatsoever.

Lying to a sea anchor

This is the traditional method of riding out a storm and without question is one of the easiest and safest. However, it does not find favour with many seasoned ocean skippers for modern yachts generally do not lie as kindly to a sea anchor as did their larger, square-rigged sisters. Nevertheless, sea anchors are an important part of any boat's survival gear and can be either simply made in the form of a drogue from canvas or similar material, or may be of a patented brand, manufactured from metal or fibreglass and specially designed with innovative features.

The sea anchor must be of suitable size and construction for the size of boat as must the length and size of the warp, which is as important here as it is with any form of ground anchor. This is where a major problem can arise, for commercially made sea anchors are rarely big enough to hold the boat firmly in position, and she tends to drift astern, creating problems in terms of taking the seas comfortably on the bow, and also in terms of creating enormous stresses on, and often causing damage to, the rudder.

It is not possible here to be specific on the size, construction or design of the sea anchor as they come in all shapes and sizes. Much depends on the experience and preference of the boat-owner, the size and weight of the boat and convenience of stowage. The traditional sea anchor is a canvas drogue with a wide circular mouth tapering to a relatively small, circular exit. This ensures that when the anchor is dragged through the water it will create considerable resistance along the warp, thus holding the boat firmly, but reasonably gently, in position.

By so doing it prevents the severe jerk of the boat bringing up to a ground anchor yet reduces the drift to a minimal amount. It will hold the boat's bow into the wind, yet allow it to ride back and absorb the sudden impact of a big, cresting wave. Patent sea anchors have much the same effect, sometimes using adjustable vanes to cater for differing sea conditions. A traditional sea anchor would need to be not less than 2 metres across the mouth for an average yacht, and this can create problems of stowage as well as streaming.

While there are a number of different ways of using a sea anchor when riding out a blow, the one described here is the recognised method for holding the vessel in a comfortable riding position to wind and wave through severe storm conditions. Once again, this refers only to traditional drogue-type sea anchors, and if a patent anchor is used, the maker's instructions for use should be followed.

129

As the storm intensifies and the wind increases, a decision must be made as to when the sails will be taken in and the sea anchor streamed. Since this equipment is mostly used only with the vessel under bare poles or a stabilising sail, the decision to furl the sails should not be left too late or the physical act of streaming the anchor, as well as taking in the sails, can become very hazardous for the crew.

There is no specific method for streaming the sea anchor initially, but traditionally it is streamed from the bow. There are schools of thought which have it streamed from other points along the hull, even from the stern and in some cases these may be acceptable. Certainly they reduce the pressure on the rudder,

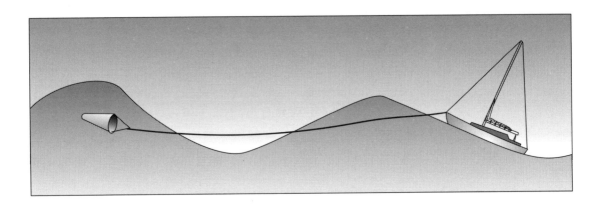

Depending on the size of the waves, the longer the warp the better; certainly the anchor should be several wave crests away from the boat. The sea anchor must be buried deep in a wave when the boat brings up against an oncoming seas.

mentioned earlier. But these can only apply in normal situations where storm conditions are developing. When the boat is to ride out the full fury of a storm on a sea anchor, it us probably best streamed from the bow.

Some experienced skippers favour streaming it from the stern, and there are some very divided opinions on this. The traditionalists point out that a boat is designed to go bow-first into the waves, not stern first. When she is running before a sea, the waves come up under her stern and carry the hull forward, thus absorbing the impact of the wave striking the stern and reducing the risk of the wave boarding over the transom. But if the boat were held in position, and the impact of the wave was not absorbed, the onrushing sea would crash over the transom and fill the cockpit every time.

Streaming a sea anchor from the stern creates just this situation; it holds the boat firmly against the oncoming wave, preventing the shock-absorbing surge forward and causing the full impact of the wave to strike the transom and pour aboard. With such a situation, the boat will be well and truly pooped by almost every wave. With the sea anchor streamed from forward, it is the bow that is pulled firmly into the waves, and since this is the way the boat is designed, the seas will

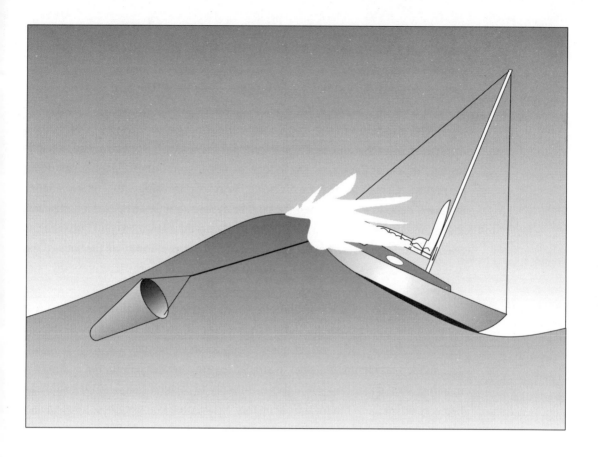

part down each side of the hull instead of pouring aboard. Even if they board, the foredeck is intended to cater for boarding seas, and there is far less risk to the boat than when a boarding sea fills the cockpit.

The other school maintains that few modern yachts ride comfortably to a sea anchor because of their underwater design-that the boat's head is either jerked severely into the waves or falls off, leaving the beam of the boat exposed to the full onslaught of each sea. This, plus the risk of damage to the rudder mentioned earlier, puts too much stress on the hull and also makes life on board much more uncomfortable.

The question of which method is correct can only be resolved by each individual boat. As mentioned earlier, no two boats react the same way to riding in a big seaway and, in most cases, only trial and error will indicate which is the most comfortable method to adopt. Suffice it to say that for the purpose of the instruction contained in this book on the techniques for streaming a sea anchor, the traditional method is adopted, although not necessarily endorsed.

The sea anchor is prepared and streamed from the bow, with the boat falling back on the warp. However, if it is more comfortable to do so it can be streamed

If the boat is held by the sea anchor, and the impact of the wave is not absorbed, the onrushing sea will crash over the transom and fill the cockpit.

131

from the cockpit, although it is important to ensure that the warp does not get under the boat and foul the propeller or rudder during this manoeuvre. When sufficient warp has been streamed, it is then taken forward and snubbed up on the forward bollard or sampson post before the weight comes on it. The boat will then bring up head to wind and sea as the slack is taken up.

The question of how much warp to let out is also the subject of many a discussion in yacht clubs and waterfront pubs. Generally speaking, and depending on the size of the waves, the longer the better; certainly the anchor should be several wave crests away from the boat. The important thing is that the sea anchor is buried deep in a wave when the boat brings up against an oncoming seas and the strain comes on the warp. In order to obtain the maximum performance the anchor should be located in the main part of a wave, preferably on the back of the wave or in its crest. The deeper it lies in the wave, the more effectively the boat will be held.

It may take a little trial and error until the boat settles down into the most comfortable riding position, but it is worth the effort, for not only will the sea anchor work more efficiently if it is properly located, but the boat will ride easier. The sudden taking up of a slack warp can create a severe jerk on the bow as the boat breasts a wave, and while this is unlikely to damage the yacht, it will make life very uncomfortable for the occupants. When properly streamed, a sea anchor provides secure and comfortable conditions in which to ride out a blow.

The use of an oil bag is favoured by many experienced skippers. A small canvas bag filled with oil is secured to the sea anchor and perforated with a needle. The slow seepage of oil spreads surprisingly far across the waves and reduces the surface chop considerably. From the bag on the sea anchor it is carried back by the waves, so that by the time it reaches the boat the seas will have flattened and eased, making life more comfortable for those on board. This technique is not as environmentally unfriendly as it sounds, for the oil used is fish oil and therefore there is no pollution problem.

While on the subject of using oil to break the severity of the waves, it is worth noting that there are other methods of spreading the oil which are as effective as the oil bag attached to the sea anchor, and can be used at times when the sea anchor is not in use.

When the boat is lying ahull, for example, is a good time to use oil, for while it does nothing to reduce the big swell which creates most of the discomfort on board, it does modify the effect of the wind waves or chop on top of the swell. The constant slap and bump of these smaller, but still sizeable wind waves can add measurably to the discomfort of living in the tossing hull of a boat riding out a storm, so any reduction in their effect is welcome.

The easiest and most effective way to spread oil across the surface of the water is by pumping it through the overside discharge of the toilet. This avoids the need to go on deck, yet provides an efficient discharge of oil at surface level. As the boat is drifting downwind, the oil spreads to windward, thus breaking the surface waves before they strike the hull.

If the toilet does not have an overside discharge then the galley sink or any other discharge pipe can be used, but as these are fairly small in diameter, the amount of oil pumped through is rather restricted. Another alternative is to use an oil-filled bag, similar to that attached to the sea anchor, suspended over the weather side, where it will seep gently, moderating the effect of the oncoming waves.

As mentioned earlier, oil is only effective in reducing the severity of surface waves and has no effect on the ground swell which is the main source of problems (and discomfort) when riding out a blow. The swells originate many hundreds of sea miles away and build as the storm builds, so little can be done on the spot to reduce their size or shape. The best that could be hoped for would be that if the swells are cresting and breaking, the oil might reduce the steepness of the crest or modify the turbulence of the break.

But the wind waves on the surface, which in themselves can build to quite a considerable size and rear steeply, creating considerable discomfort, are much easier to tame. They succumb readily to the surface oil, losing their ferocity and steepness and flowing more gently down the side of the hull. Try emptying the oil from a tin of sardines over the side when at anchor in harbour one day; the effect on the surface wind waves will readily illustrate how effective this system is for making life a little easier when riding out big seas.

Running before the wind

This method of riding out a storm is effective providing the blow is not too strong, but it is fairly demanding on both boat and crew. It can only be carried out under certain conditions and needs a skilled hand at the tiller. Sometimes sail is carried, but in severe conditions the method is undertaken with only bare poles; the effect of the wind on the rigging being sufficient to give the boat steerage. Mostly, a tiny storm or spitfire jib is the choice, for this has insufficient area to create strong wind resistance, yet will give the boat better steerage and control.

The conditions which make running before the wind and sea a practical proposition are basically:

1.   wind not too strong;
2.   seas not too big (particularly not too steep);
3.   a well-designed ocean-going boat, preferably with a canoe stern;
4.   a strong, well-secured rudder;
5.   plenty of sizeable rope warps;
6.   a skilled helmsman; and
7.   plenty of sea room.

Running before the wind and sea is usually a technique adopted fairly early in the storm because as the wind and seas increase in strength and size it can become more difficult to carry out and more demanding on the crew. As the storm increases a decision must be made whether or not to adopt one of the other methods, or use this method to ride out the full fury of the storm. As with other methods, this depends to a certain extent on the way the boat behaves, but a well-found, ocean-going boat with a fairly long keel should not encounter too many problems, even in a big blow.

Running before the wind and sea is a popular method when the sea is moderate. As the seas increase, the stress on boat and crew can become much more intensive.

Assuming the storm to be developing and the boat tacking to windward, there comes a point where the sails must be reefed and the boat made more comfortable. If the storm continues to increase, further reefing or some other technique can be employed to ease the pressure. But as time goes on and the wind becomes stronger, there will be a point at which it is no longer practical to continue driving ahead. The boat must abandon her original course and settle down to riding it out.

Providing there is plenty of sea room, this is the time to let her head pay off and under a small spitfire jib or something similar, run before the wind, taking both wind and waves on an angle to the quarter. The small headsail provides stability and helps steering, while keeping the seas on the quarter prevents either an unexpected broach or and untimely gybe. Either of these can cause the boat to slew across the seas and make for considerable discomfort; there is even the danger of rolling over if the seas are big enough.

There are other factors to bear in mind, too, such as the enormous strain on the rudder and the need for a well-shaped stern, which will prevent the pile-up of sea astern from boarding and pooping the yacht. As a general rule, most well-found, ocean-going craft can cope with these stresses, but if there is any doubt, then this method of riding it out should be abandoned in favour of lying ahull or using a sea anchor. This is the time when the earlier cautious approach to purchasing the right boat for the job pays off.

Another factor that must be considered when running before the seas is the enormous stress on the helmsman. Rarely is it possible for the helm to be lashed or secured, even for a brief period, as this will invite the seas to board or the boat to broach. And self-steering devices often cannot cope with these conditions, so the helm must be handled physically. The skill of the helmsman is put very much to the test under these conditions, in keeping the boat heading down the waves and preventing her from yawing too far one way or the other. There is probably no other time in the course of an ocean or coastal passage when the helmsman's experience and skill will be called on to such an extent. A mistake here can mean disaster with a capital D.

One method of easing the stress on both the helm and the helmsman is to stream warps. These are long ropes of good diameter which can be run out from the stern of the boat, either in a bight or loose ended, or even with a very small drogue or bucket on the end. The dragging effect of these warps tends to steady the boat and take some of the stress from the steering. The drag on the stern reduces the tendency of the waves to push the hull to one side or another, which is the key factor in inducing an unwanted broach. By reducing this tendency the effort required to hold the boat on course is also reduced, thus taking much of the strain from the rudder and in turn easing the load on the helmsman.

The use of a small bucket or drogue can be very effective, but it is important that this piece of equipment is not too large, creating too much drag, or it will have the reverse effect to that required. As mentioned when describing the dangers of using a sea anchor from the stern, if the boat is pulled up short when running before a sea, there is every possibility of the wave boarding over the transom and this is a very unhealthy condition. A small drogue or bucket will create extra drag, but

135

not pull the boat up short, so this will maximise the effect of the warps and make steering much easier.

The small spitfire jib described earlier can also have the same effect of assisting the steering, but as the wind increases there is a possibility that any sail at all may be too much and the boat is better running under bare poles with warps streamed astern. When properly set up this is often the most comfortable position in which to ride out a blow, but the strain on the helmsman and the increasing risk of broaching as the seas grow in size, usually means that in a gale of extreme severity or length one of the other, less strenuous methods of riding it out may need to be employed.

Which is the safest and most suitable method to use will depend on the circumstances that exist at the time, the experience of the crew and the size and shape of the boat's hull. Of these, as already mentioned, experience is the major factor, for a boat is only as good as the crew that handle her and while most well-found vessels will survive any storm, inexperience and incorrect handling can put even those vessels at risk. Previous experience in riding out a gale at sea with a tried and tested boat is the best insurance against problems when things turn nasty.

Riding it out in a motor yacht

Motor yachts are not used widely for ocean crossing for a number of reasons, not least of which are the long distances involved, the limited amount of fuel that can be carried and the lack of conveniently spaced refuelling stations. So it is unlikely that a powered vessel would be caught out in a blow in the middle of an ocean. Also, a major advantage of having big motors in the hull is the ability to outrun an approaching storm by making it into shelter before the blow gets under way. Of course, the factors inhibiting a yacht's attempts to run inshore for shelter also apply to powered vessels, but once again the speed factor usually makes it possible to get into a harbour or bay before the dangerous coastal sea conditions build up.

So the most likely scenario where a motor yacht has to ride out a blow would be in waters that are relatively close to shore, but where the opportunity to run for shelter either does not exist, or storm conditions develop at such a speed that it is safer to stay out at sea. The skipper and crew of a powered vessel must then prepare for the oncoming gale in just the same basic way as the crew of a sailing yacht, although there are a few major differences between the two types of vessels which must be born in mind.

Firstly, the nature of the hull design of most powered craft makes them

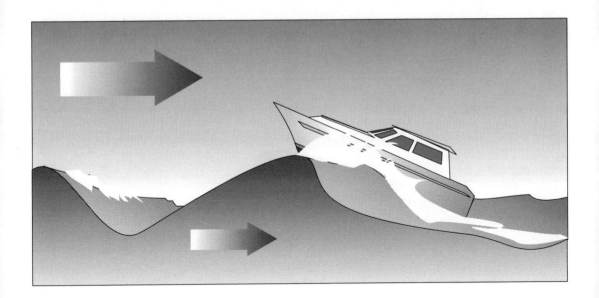

vulnerable to capsize. Lacking the ballast of a deep keeled yacht, and the beam of a multihull, a power-driven vessel can be easily rolled over in a seaway, and in most cases will not be self-righting. This obviously places limitations on the methods that can be adopted for riding out a storm. Lying ahull, for example, is a very risky procedure. Since the boat is likely to lie broadside to the wind and seas, the possibility of capsize is very real and this method should not be attempted.

Running before the sea can work, although here again there is a degree of risk, depending to a great extent on the amount of power (and thus speed) the boat can produce in order to run with the seas. A common practice in crossing a bar is to 'ride' the back of a wave, using the throttle to control the boat's position and prevent her running over the crest or falling back under the following wave. This is quite a good practice although maintaining this situation for some time, as would be the case when running before a storm, would be very taxing on both boat and helmsman.

Initially, the boat should be held to wind and sea with the motors. Assuming there is no possibility of making it to shelter, she should be rounded up and headed into the seas, with the throttle adjusted to hold the boat in the most comfortable position. Of course, if the blow continues for any length of time, this can create problems of its own, for apart from the discomfort, sooner or later the fuel is going to run out and then disaster can move in. However, if the blow is likely to be of short duration, holding her head to sea on the motors is the best move initially. If the blow continues, another method must be brought into play.

Assuming there is no possibility of making it to shelter, the boat should be rounded up and headed into the seas, with the throttle adjusted to hold the boat in the most comfortable position.

137

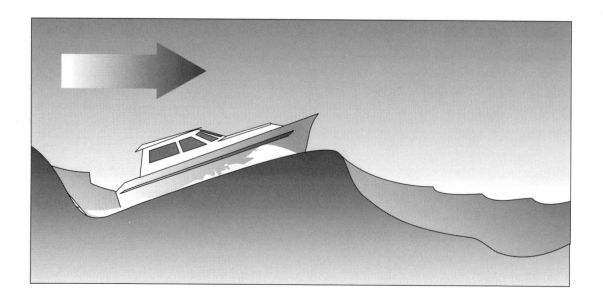

A common practice in crossing a bar is to 'ride' the back of a wave.

Probably the safest method of riding it out is with a sea anchor streamed. The boat is then held in position with her bow to the seas where there is little likelihood of her swinging beam-on and capsizing. This is a fairly safe and comfortable position and if the sea anchor is set correctly, could be a satisfactory means of riding out even a long blow. Of course, all the procedures described for lying to a sea anchor in a yacht must be observed. If close to the coast there needs to be good sea room to leeward.

A lee shore can be just as dangerous for a power boat as for a sailing vessel, although if the shore gets too close, using motors to get the boat away from danger is much easier than trying to sail off to windward. Other than this, the length of the warp, the use of an oil bag, and other factors involved in riding to a sea anchor are no different to those employed by a sailing vessel.

CHAPTER 10

When the chips are down

Despite all the precautions, the good seamanship, the sound boat and the experience, there can still come a time when the boat is suddenly precipitated into dangerous situation. It may be the result of an unfortunate accident, an unforeseen development or a mishap that could neither have been anticipated nor prevented.

It can be the result of misjudgement, either of the weather, or the boat's ability handle a big sea, or perhaps of a navigational error which puts the boat into a vulnerable position in relation to a coastline or offlying dangers; sea room is of vital importance in riding out a blow. Misjudgement of the onset or movement of the storm, or of its intensity could be other reasons why the boat, despite all precautions, finds herself in a dangerous, potentially fatal situation.

It could also, of course, be the result of the elements becoming just too much and overwhelming the boat with sheer ferocity or unmanageable conditions. This can be the case with cyclones, typhoons, hurricanes and other tropical storms. Caught in the eye of such a storm, few yachts have much chance of survival. Since soundly constructed shore establishments can be easily demolished by such storms, and giant ocean-going ships can succumb, relatively fragile small craft caught out at sea have next to no chance.

Whatever the reason, when a boat finds herself in such a situation, drastic action must be taken if she and her crew are to survive. Such action can be instinctive or an established survival practice, depending on the conditions of the emergency and the skill of the crew.

The forms of danger which can overtake an ocean-going yacht in storm conditions are many and varied, and countering them will call on every fibre of skill that experience the crew can muster. Much of this will be instinctive, born of long years of close association with the sea. But there are some basic procedures which have been developed as the result of experience and which, when the chips are down, can mean the difference between life and death, between disaster and survival. Every sailor should be aware of these against the chance that one day, despite all precautions, the relatively simple practices for riding out a storm go wrong and the boat is thrown into danger.

Treacherous lee shore

Few situations at sea create such a severe problem as being blown down on a lee shore. It was the nemesis of the old salts in the windjammers of yesteryear and still haunts the seagoing adventurer of today. Nothing is more calculated to strike fear into the heart of any seaman than the proximity of a dangerous lee shore. Sailing craft are most vulnerable because they have to 'claw' their way into the wind to get away from it, but even powered vessels are at risk, since a motor failure on a lee shore leaves the boat with only one direction to drift-into disaster.

Nothing is more calculated to strike fear into the heart of any seaman than the proximity of a dangerous lee shore.

The old windjammers were particularly vulnerable because their rig made it hard for them to work to windward and, once on a lee shore, few were able to regain the safety of the open sea. The lee shores of the world (onto which the prevailing winds blow) are littered with wrecks of these old ships, in stark contrast

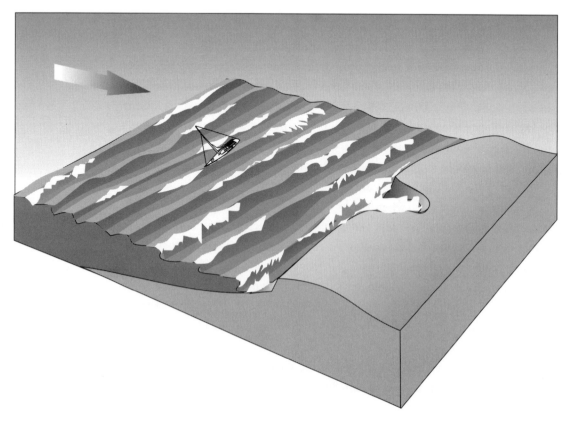

to the weather shores, where only the odd wreck will be found. While steamships and motor-powered vessels fared a little better, there are still many of their bones in these graveyards, for it takes only one mistake and the demonic combination of strong wind and lee shore can quickly claim another victim.

The obvious answer to the problem is that the boat should never be close to a lee shore, but that is easier said than done and is rather akin to telling a pedestrian he should never cross a road because the traffic creates a dangerous situation. There are times when the pedestrian *must* cross the road, and similarly it would be impossible to sail all the time along a coast with a weather shore.

More to the point, a boat that is caught in a storm, perhaps hundreds of miles from any lee shore, can at some stage find herself inexorably blow down on that lee shore, either as a result of running before the seas or drifting to leeward while lying ahull or hove to. A storm at sea can take many days to pass, and in that time a yacht, while riding it out quite confidently, can drift long distances, and a shoreline which was well out of calculation at the time the blow set in, can become a problem before the storm has blown itself out.

The danger then is exacerbated because, with a gale still blowing, it may be difficult, even impossible, to get the boat under way and haul her off the approaching lee shore. If storm sails can be set or a motor fired up, then the chances are she will gain enough forward momentum to slowly make progress into the wind and increase the distance between the boat and the looming breakers along the shoreline. But if the wind is too strong then the sails may aggravate the situation and the motor simply raise false hopes. Heeling excessively under the pressure of the sails may cause the boat to drift downwind rather than make progress into the wind. Also, she may become unmanageable with wind and sea pushing her bow away constantly and again bringing that dangerous shore closer rather than widening the precious stretch of sea to leeward.

If this situation exists, or the boat is unable to carry any sail or make headway with the motor, then the emergency requires drastic survival measures. It is unlikely assistance can be called from shore or any other source, although obviously a call for help should be put out on all emergency channels. But in the big seas that exist under storm conditions, even the arrival of assistance may not solve the problem. Rescue vessels will have difficulty getting a tow aboard without placing themselves in danger and the best that can be hoped for in an extreme situation would be that either rescue craft or helicopters would be able to get the crew off.

So the best chances of survival rest with the boat itself and the crew. And the only survival equipment which will be effective under these conditions will be the ground anchor. The sea anchor, despite its usefulness in deeper waters, is

When close to a lee shore, the only survival equipment which will be effective will be the ground anchor. An extra long warp will be necessary.

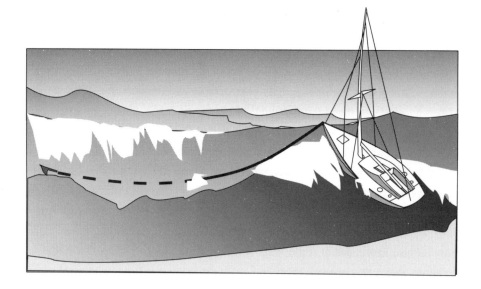

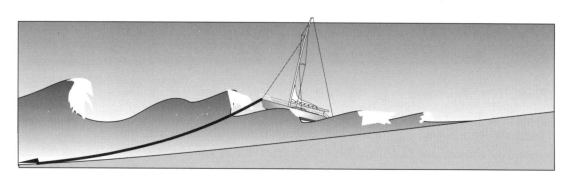

There is an old maxim that the longer the anchor warp the better the chances of the anchor holding

pointless here as it allows the boat to drift to leeward, and on a lee shore there is no room to drift astern. The heaviest ground anchor aboard should be prepared with all the chain the boat carries, and this secured to a warp consisting of every metre of rope that can be found. There is an old maxim that the longer the anchor warp the better the chances of the anchor holding, so every centimetre of the original anchor warp, plus spare lines, sheets, and every length of line that can be found on board, must be pressed into service.

There is no room for any refined techniques here; the anchor is lowered and the improvised warp paid out to its full length before being secured around the sampson post at the bow. It is more than likely the anchor will not touch bottom, depending on the distance from the lee shore and the depth of the water in the area. But it is nevertheless secured in position so that as the boat drifts into shallower water, the anchor hopefully will snag the bottom and hold the boat before the shore is reached. If the water is sufficiently shallow some distance out from the shore, then there is a good chance of the anchor digging in and holding before the boat gets even close to the breakers.

142

Digging in is one thing, holding the boat against the wind and sea is another, and the battle is by no means over even if the anchor holds. But it does offer a respite and, if conditions are really extreme, a chance for rescue vessels or helicopters to get the crew off. If luck holds and the anchor does not break out, there may be no need for rescue and the boat may be able to ride out the rest of the storm on the ground tackle. However, being anchored on a lee shore is a situation fraught with danger, and the crew will be constantly haunted by the thought that if at any stage the anchor pulls out, the boat will drift back onto the waiting lee shore, with dire consequences for both boat and crew. It is definitely not the most comfortable of anchorages even in good conditions.

Without outside help there is no alternative and since the entire anchor warp is out, there is nothing more that can be done other than, perhaps, pray! At least the immediate situation is relieved and if the crew's luck and the anchor both hold, the discomfort of the anchorage will be offset by the fact that when the wind dies, the emergency will ease.

Beaching the boat

If the anchor does not hold, or for some other reason the boat's drift towards the lee shore cannot be arrested, then a different survival technique will be called for.

If the coastline consists of rocky cliffs dropping into deep, turbulent water, then the chips are really down and nothing short of divine intervention will save either boat or crew. However, if the shoreline offers a beach or some less horrendous seascape than the cliffs, then there is a chance that even though the boat is lost, the crew might survive. Hopefully they are good swimmers, for their ability in this regard will be sorely tested.

There are many theories on how best this emergency can be met, much depending on the conditions that exist and the type of boat involved. Even without sail, most yachts retain a certain amount of steerage when being blown through the water, but it may be necessary to set a small jib in order to gain some control. With steerage, the boat can be headed towards the beach and away from any nearby dangers such as offlying reefs. When closing with the outer line of breakers, the crew must prepare to abandon ship, donning life-jackets if they are not already worn.

Now much depends on the boat and her equipment. If an inflatable raft is carried, it should be inflated and jettisoned on the end of a line. This will provide flotation either with the crew scrambling into the raft and riding it through the surf or hanging on to the life-lines around the outside. The skipper, manoeuvring the

143

Steerage when beaching through the surf can be a problem, for it is important the boat does not slew broadside to the seas. A small jib is often all that is required to give her steerage.

yacht close to the surf, can set her on course across the waves, then join the crew in the water, casting off the life-raft as he abandons the yacht. The raft will give a very uncomfortable ride in through the surf and create a particularly difficult situation for those hanging on to the life-lines. But it will provide a buoyant platform which, together with their life-jackets, should enable the crew to make their way through the surf to the beach with a fair chance of survival.

Another school of thought suggests that the crew ride the yacht into the surf and stay with her until she beaches herself in the broken water, at which point they abandon her and make for the beach. This can work, but there is a very real danger that as the yacht is carried into the breaking surf, she will hit bottom and roll over, creating extreme danger of injury to any crew who are not quick to abandon ship, or who may already be in the water.

Even without the life-raft, abandoning the yacht outside the break and leaving her to beach herself in the surf some distance away eliminates this danger to the crew, who will have enough problems getting through the surf break to the shore without the added hazard of a berserk yacht thrashing around in her death throes on top of them.

Abandon ship!

Although there will be times such as that described above when all else fails and there is no alternative but to abandon the yacht, this should only be done as an absolutely last resort. A dangerous lee shore when the anchor will not hold is just such a case, for close inshore there is nowhere for the boat to go but into the white water. Well out at sea, with plenty of room, however, abandoning ship should be avoided until there is no possible alternative, because the chances of survival are always better staying with the yacht than leaving her.

This was graphically illustrated in the tragic Fastnet Race of 1979 when the cream of the world's yachting fleets were decimated by a freak storm that resulted in fifteen crewmen losing their lives. The inquiry which followed the tragedy indicated that a number of yachts which had been abandoned were still afloat and were recovered long after the incident was over. Some of their crews were among those drowned, and it would appear that had those crews stayed with their boats, there would have been every chance that they would have survived.

As long as the boat is afloat, she is a survival platform; albeit a wet, uncomfortable and perhaps risky platform. But she is still a survival platform, and only when it is obvious that she is about to take her final plunge should she be abandoned. Traditional fears of being 'sucked down' by a sinking ship do not apply to small craft, although there is of course a danger of getting caught in the rigging, so the time to abandon must be determined to enable all crew to get safely clear.

Precautions should be taken so that when the time comes, the abandoning procedure goes smoothly and efficiently. A life-raft should be inflated, prepared and tied to the stern, provisions placed aboard where necessary, and radio contact with shore stations or other craft maintained to the last moment so a positive fix on the boat's position can be passed to rescue craft. The actual moment of abandoning should still be postponed until there is no further hope of saving the boat, for even a waterlogged hull can remain afloat for a surprisingly long time. The old maxim of 'stay with the boat' holds good as much with ocean-going craft as it does with any other.

The international distress call MAYDAY transmitted on any radio frequency will immediately alert all ship and shore stations within range, and the message will be quickly passed to search and rescue co-ordinators. MAYDAY can only be used for extreme emergencies (when there is immediate danger of loss of life) and abandoning a sinking yacht would classify as just such an emergency. The skipper should have trained his crew in handling such distress transmissions, for in a crisis situation the skipper may himself be incapacitated, so every person on board should be capable of sending a MAYDAY signal.

When the life-raft is finally cast off, it will hopefully be only a matter of time before rescue arrives. Having maintained radio contact with rescue co-ordinators and kept a regular plot on the boat's position, there should be no problem in ships or aircraft finding the life-raft, and the regular transmission of EPIRB signals will help pinpoint its position. There is only need to use one EPIRB at a time, even if more than one are carried; best to retain any unused transmitters in case rescue is slow and the batteries of the first EPIRB run low.

Much the same applies to the use of rockets, flares and other visual signalling equipment. They should not be used unless there is a very high likelihood of their being seen by searching vessels. A flare or rocket is often hard to spot from a searching aircraft unless it is in close proximity to the survivors. Firing off all the visual signals at the first sound of a searching aircraft may mean there will be none left when the rescuers are close and there is a far better chance of the signals being seen.

A life-raft is a very difficult object to pick on a wide, wind-blown sea, either from the air or from searching vessels, and for this reason, visual signals are important. By day, an orange smoke flare offers the best chance of being spotted against the blue and white of the sea, or a coloured stain which spreads through the water around the raft. By night hand-held flares are easily seen from the air, but may not be easily spotted by surface craft as the raft will frequently be hidden in the troughs. In this case, rockets carrying parachute flares have a better chance of being seen.

Probably the most important piece of emergency equipment is the EPIRB which transmits a regular signal.

Probably the most important piece of equipment at this time is the EPIRB. This transmits a regular emergency signal which can be picked up by a wide variety of rescue organisations, even by commercial aircraft on their normal flight paths. Even more importantly, modern EPIRB signals can be picked up by satellite monitors which relay the signals directly to rescue co-ordination centres. This enables the location of the raft to be pinpointed with remarkable accuracy anywhere on the global sea. No yacht of any kind should put to sea without at EPIRB on board.

Adrift on the ocean

Modern life-rafts are mostly self-contained capsules that provide secure shelter and reasonable safety for survivors adrift on the open sea. Providing all the correct procedures have been followed, contact has been made with rescue services and an EPIRB is beeping away, it should be only a matter of time before help is at hand. Unfortunately the best laid plans can go very much astray and even the most experienced and competent crew can find themselves adrift with no prospect of rescue for some time.

This is usually the result of failure to communicate with the outside world before the yacht sinks and the crew take to the raft. Happily, modern satellite communications offer a good back-up by pinpointing a beeping EPIRB surprisingly accurately, so even if the crew failed to make contact while the boat was afloat, the satellite will alert rescue headquarters of the situation. But of course, even then rescue may be difficult if the raft is drifting out of range of rescue craft and away from shipping routes. While no doubt a rescue will be effected sooner or later, a crew cast adrift in the middle of the ocean may well find that they will be spending some considerable time in the life-raft before help arrives.

While inflatable life-rafts are very safe emergency craft, they are not the most comfortable and life cooped up beneath the canopy will be unpleasant even in a relatively quiet sea. If the yacht was abandoned at the height of a gale, the cork-like action of the raft in a big sea will make life on board almost unbearable. Even the strongest seafaring stomachs succumb to seasickness under these conditions, which in turn does not improve the humid, fetid atmosphere inside the raft.

Just before abandoning the yacht, emergency supplies should be placed aboard the raft and supplemented with anything that might help reduce the misery of being cast adrift. Depending on the size of the raft, the number of people in it and the time available for preparing it before the yacht sank, it is often possible

Modern satellites can pinpoint a beeping EPIRB surprisingly accurately.

to carry quite a considerable amount of emergency items.

The most important, of course, are water, food, signalling equipment and a first aid box. Given space, the emergency rations can be supplemented with tins or dried food from the boat; a decent meal, albeit from a tin, can do wonders for morale when the crew are down in the dumps awaiting rescue that never seems to come. Likewise, if there was time before abandoning the yacht, hot thermoses of tea, coffee or soup can help, particularly in temperate or cold climates.

Clothing is also important. The chances are the crew will eat, drink and sleep in wet clothing, and little can be done about this, but warm clothing, even wet, can be a life-saver. When the storm abates there may be a chance to dry things out a little, so spare clothes, if they can be carried in plastic bags, offer a change from soaked, salty gear, even if only for a short period. Naturally, all these extras are conditional upon there being room in the raft and time to put them together before the yacht foundered.

A drogue, usually supplied as part of the raft, will reduce drift and stabilise the raft, although it will do little to reduce the discomfort which is an unavoidable part of any survival situation. But with a reasonable supply of food and water, and with rescue services aware of the problem, the chances of survival are fairly high. Keeping the EPIRB working is of prime importance and once the search begins it will be this little piece of equipment which will probably mean the difference between survival and disaster.

Rescue by helicopter

The liferaft (or man in the water) must be allowed to drift well clear of the stricken vessel to avoid risk of the helicopter or the winch line fouling the mast or rigging.

The use of helicopters in rescue operations where yachts are concerned has introduced a new angle to rescue techniques. The wildly gyrating mast of a stricken yacht can create a formidable hazard to a helicopter attempting to lift crew from the deck. Apart from the likelihood of the chopper rotors striking the mast or rigging, there is also the risk of the winch line becoming entangled in the rigging as the crew are winched upwards from the deck. Either mishap could endanger the chopper, the yacht and both crews.

To avoid this, a life-raft must be prepared prior to the start of a helicopter rescue. The first of the crew is placed in the life-raft and allowed to drift astern for some distance on the end of a line. The helicopter pilot can now manoeuvre his craft safely into position over the raft and winch a survivor up without risk of either the chopper or the survivor coming into contact with the boat's rigging.

The raft is then hauled back along its line and loaded with a second crew member and the procedure repeated. When all crew have been winched to safety,

the yacht and the raft are abandoned. Of course, if the yacht has already sunk and the crew must be rescued from the raft, the mast and rigging problem does not exist.

If the boat does not have a raft or dinghy in which the crew can be dropped astern, then each will have to jump into the water and swim clear of the yacht on the end of a safety line. The chopper will then drop a man down on the end of the winch cable to assist with the rescue, or lower a sling into which the survivor in the water can climb. The hook of the winch cable should be allowed to touch the sea to discharge any static electricity that it may contain. It is important to ensure that each person in the water is attached to the yacht by a safety line so that they can get back aboard if the helicopter rescue is not successful. The safety line can be released as soon as the helicopter winch harness is secure.

A flooded hull

One of the most common causes of emergency at sea is the flooding of the hull. This may come about in a number of ways, some of which have been described earlier. Windows or hatches which are stove in will allow access to large volumes of water, as will broken skin fittings or damaged pipes. Less common, but still sometimes experienced, is puncturing of the hull skin. This can come about as a result of the boat striking something in the water; not uncommon in shipping lanes where large items of flotsam are frequently encountered. The hull can also be punctured by spars or gear that falls over the side when the boat is dismasted.

Whatever the cause, the result is fast flooding of the hull through a hole in the skin, and this must be plugged urgently or the boat will be in danger of foundering. A hole which is reasonably round can often be closed using one of the cone-shaped plugs that are a standard part of any boat's emergency equipment. Such plugs, when selected to suit the size of the hole and hammered home firmly, will stem the flow until more permanent repairs can be made. As a rule the plugs are made of timber and therefore suit any hull material. No boat should put to sea without a selection of such wooden plugs on board.

If the hole is too large to close in this way, a more substantial plug will need to be made. Rolled up canvas, pillows, even mattresses, can be rammed into the hole to stop the flow. Naturally, all such plugs are temporary and some sort of patching or repair job will be necessary as quickly as possible to make the hull sound again. But at least these temporary plugs will stem the flow of water and, at this stage and with this type of damage, stemming the flow is the difference between the boat staying afloat and sinking.

To keep a large, temporary plug in place while the boat continues to pound her way through the waves will probably need one of the crew permanently holding it in position on the inside. An alternative (or extra) measure is to place a sail around the outside of the hull, covering the damage, but this is a very difficult exercise in storm conditions, and often not very successful, as the wallowing of the boat in the seas makes it almost impossible to secure the sail in position.

However, even desperate measures must be used when the situation is serious, and in any case, as conditions moderate, the sail around the hull can provide a quite effective means of preventing the plug being pushed out, or reducing the amount of water getting in. It is rarely a success on its own, as it cannot be secured tightly enough to the hull, but in conjunction with a plug of some type, can help to reduce the danger of the boat filling with water.

The bucket brigade

When the hull is flooded, bilge pumps are rarely very effective in reducing the inflow of water. Designed mainly to cope with the small amounts of water encountered in normal use, these pumps, while useful, do not usually have sufficient capacity to cope with serious flooding. They should be used of course, for every little helps, but usually the crew can be used more efficiently in the form of a bucket brigade. Buckets can move a great deal of water very quickly if they

A bucket brigade that is well organised with a number of crew can reduce the water level in the hull faster than any bilge pump.

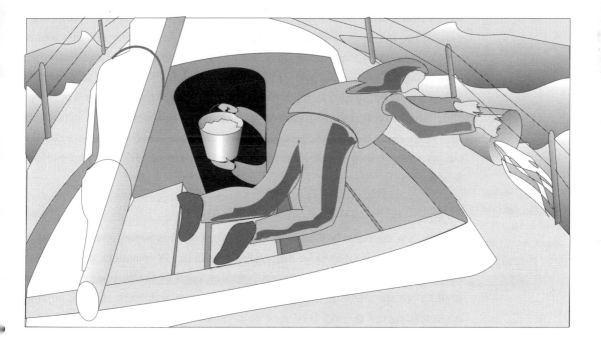

are used productively, and a well-organised bucket brigade can soon reduce a flooded hull from a near-terminal state to a survival platform state, and when the chips are down, a survival platform is all that is required.

The bucket brigade format differs from boat to boat, but basically consists of one or two crew members down below forming a chain gang with another crew member in the companionway and another in the cockpit. Fast scooping with the buckets down below and smooth, efficient chain-gang handling passing the buckets into the cockpit, emptying them and returning them below, is the essence of success with the bucket brigade. The effect on the water in the hull will be quite dramatic unless the boat is still flooding badly, but with a patch or plug reducing the inflow, and a well-organised bucket team removing the water with a smooth, efficient motion, it should not take long to return the boat to a state of reasonably safety.

The bucket brigade can then be reduced to perhaps one or two persons, who can hold the reduced inflow and keep the flooding in check. Providing there is not too much water still coming in, the bilge pumps may be able to cope with it, and pumping can be less demanding on the crew than swinging full buckets around.

Dismasting

This is perhaps the most common type of problem encountered by ocean-going yachts, especially in storm conditions. It can be a fairly innocuous happening, or it can mean disaster. Losing the mast itself is not a great hazard, but it is the damage done by the falling gear that can create considerable danger. For example, a mast which lies over the side entangled in rigging is a real danger, especially in a seaway, as the broken end of the mast, or perhaps some fitting or spar, can easily punch a hole in the hull as the boat and gear wallow together in the waves.

Similarly, fittings torn out of the deck or damage to the hull or cabin from the falling gear can create holes which allow water to get below and, with the boat out of control in a seaway, this can mean danger of flooding and perhaps foundering.

It happens to the best of us! Close inshore it's not such a problem, but half way across an ocean it can create a few headaches.

The first step when the boat is dismasted, is to get rid of the fallen gear. As a general rule, the mast falls over the side and lies alongside, entangled in rigging, and this is when it can be dangerous. It must be cut away before a hole is punched in the side of the boat or some other damage is done. Wire cutters, or even better bolt cutters, should be a part of every boat's emergency toolbox and these can be used to cut the stays or shrouds and free the mast and spars. An axe, also an important part of the tool box, may be required to assist in clearing the debris.

Bigger problems arise if the rigging becomes entangled in the rudder or propeller or if, as described earlier, the hull sustains damage when the mast falls. These problems will vary according to the individual situation and can only be dealt with on an individual basis. Generally, however, quick cutting away of the rigging, allowing the mast and gear to sink, and pulling aboard any remaining gear still over the side, will resolve most problems and clear the decks for the next step.

Using jury gear

When the mast goes over the side, the main propulsion unit for the yacht has been lost and some alternative must be found in order to bring her under control and head for assistance. If the coast is reasonably close and the storm is dying, the motor may be sufficient to make it to the nearest port. But if the boat is in the middle of the ocean or the storm is still blowing strongly, the motor will be somewhat limited.

Most yachts have only small, auxiliary engines and a limited fuel capacity. While the motor may be sufficient to provide steerage way in order to ride out the storm reasonably comfortably, it is unlikely to have sufficient fuel to make a passage to the nearest coastline, or for that matter to make much progress in any direction. Some form of jury rig is necessary to give the boat steerage and, if possible, make some way through the water.

It goes without saying that the extent and sophistication of the jury rig will depend on the materials available on the boat. If the mast broke off high above the deck, then the stump will provide a good basis on which to design and rig the jury gear. Similarly, if some of the broken mast was retrieved when it was cut away from the rigging, this, too, offers a good basis on which to build a jury rig.

But if, as is often the case, the mast snapped close to the deck, then the crew has the disconcerting task of erecting a whole new mast from the step upwards. And if the entire mast section that went over the side is now lying on the sea bed, then there is not usually much on board which can be used to create a jury mast of any substance. Spinnaker poles and similar spars can be pressed into use, but these provide only a limited height onto which the jury sails can be rigged. The ingenuity of the crew may be put to the test in erecting a spar to provide a reasonable substitute mast.

For this reason, there is not a great deal that can be offered in a book such as this, by way of instruction or advice on how to rig jury gear. It is dependent almost entirely on what may be available on board and how the crew can best put it to use. A jury mast needs to be as tall as possible, but since there are few items

Almost anything can be used for jury gear, but a long spar is necessary for a jury mast if any sails are to be set.

carried on the normal yacht that are more than a few metres long, the crew will need to scratch their heads as to how best to make a mast of reasonable size with what is available, and then erect it on the stump of the old mast.

Jury sails are easier to come up with as the normal sails come in different sizes and usually a small spitfire jib or a storm tri-sail main will be at least part way suitable for the new, shortened mast. While making progress to windward may be difficult as the sails are unlikely to assume their best aerofoil shape, reaching or running with jury sails is not usually a problem.

Jury rudders are a common requirement at sea, for the rudder of modern yachts can be vulnerable in a seaway, both to the stresses of steering through a heavy sea, and also to the possibility of being fouled by fallen rigging. Whatever the cause, if the boat is without steerage and no form of emergency steering can be brought into play, a jury rudder will be required.

This is usually easier to rig than a jury mast since the length of spar required is relatively short. A long oar, if carried, might be strong enough for a small yacht, or a built structure, using a spinnaker pole and hatchway or door can be improvised to create a substitute steering oar. The shank of the oar, however constructed, must be well secured to the boat-usually by lashing to the stern pushpit-in order to give the necessary leverage to provide steering power. If well constructed and with the blade well immersed in the water, such a device can provide good steering control for even a sizeable yacht.

As mentioned earlier, any form of jury gear is totally dependent on the materials available at the time. But since a jury-rigged boat is not intended to have racing ability, but is essentially a survival platform that can, within reason, be moved, a few odd bits and pieces, together with a resourceful approach by the crew can work surprisingly well. Many a yacht has limped home under jury gear after a pasting in the open ocean, to be admired and applauded by the local seafaring fraternity.

Man overboard

There are few situations more desperate than losing a crew member overboard in the middle of a full-blown gale. Even under normal conditions, a crew member in the water in the open sea can create serious problems. Those problems are exacerbated a thousandfold when it happens in the middle of a storm. Particularly is this the case when the boat is under way, perhaps running before the storm. Getting back to rescue the person in the water can then be a herculean, if not impossible task.

First steps are obviously to avoid, wherever possible, the chances of anyone being lost overboard. Any crew member who comes up on deck when the boat is riding out a storm must wear life-jacket and harness and *secure the harness even before leaving the cabin.* It is more than feasible that the boat could take a sudden lurch or for the sea to board over the stern just as a change of watch is taking place. The new crew, having just stepped into the cockpit, could be thrown or swept overboard before they have time to clip on their harness ropes. Every seagoing boat should have some anchor point near the companionway where harnesses can be clipped on as crew climb through the hatchway into the cockpit.

Similarly, it goes without saying that any of the crew working on deck for any reason must be well secured at all times. Even during a lull or if the storm abates temporarily, harnesses must remain secured, for it requires only one small slip and disaster can follow swiftly. Particularly is this the case at night. Rescuing a person from the water in stormy conditions is a near impossible task in day-time; at night there is often no chance at all.

The method of picking up someone in the water will depend on the situation at the time. A different technique will be required if the boat is hove to, lying to a sea anchor or lying ahull, and a totally different method used if the boat is running before the storm. In the first three cases, the boat is relatively stationary and it may be possible to reach the person in the water with a light heaving line or a life-ring secured with a line. If the victim is unconscious or cannot make it back, it may be necessary to have one of the crew, secured by a life-line, swim out and make the rescue.

The biggest danger in this situation is that the person in the water drifts out of range of a thrown line or a swimming rescuer. If the boat is brought up to a sea anchor she cannot be got under way and manoeuvred round quickly and the only practical solution might be to trip or cut the anchor line and allow the boat to drift astern, hopefully to bring the person in the water within range again. In the meantime, if the motor can be started, the boat can be got under way. Much the same applies if the boat is lying ahull. Another practice in this situation is to keep a life-raft or inflatable hanging off the stern on the end of a line. Anyone falling overboard and unable to get back to the yacht may be able to grab the trailing dinghy.

If the boat is hove to, the headsail can be released and sheeted onto its correct side, which will then provide full manoeuvring power; a normal rescue routine can then be undertaken. Since this may involve a fairly wide sweep in order to bring the boat into a safe recovery position, it is essential not to lose sight of the person in the water. A dan buoy or floating flare should be released and one of the crew detailed to keep his or her eye firmly on the person in the water, as it is very easy to lose someone among the hillocks of a big sea.

If the boat is running before a sea with warps out astern, the situation can be very serious. While she can be brought up to wind and the sails sheeted on fairly quickly, she will not handle well with the warps still trailing astern. Designed to create drag, they will make it virtually impossible for the boat to be manoeuvred back towards the person in the water, and hauling in the warps will lose valuable time. Once again, releasing a dan buoy or flare and stationing a look-out to keep the victim in sight is essential while the warps are being brought in and the boat got under way, after which normal man overboard drills can be followed.

There are many other ideas and techniques on what to do when a person falls overboard, and they are doubtless all fine in theory. But in the practical situation of a crew member overboard in a big seaway at the height of a howling gale, theories are often difficult to translate into solutions. The 'common practice of seamanship' as it is termed in legal jargon, is the basis of any successful action when a person goes over the side, and often set techniques will not work where ingenuity and experience will.

Index